BAD NEWS IN BANGKOK

The Bucky Stone Series

1. *Making Waves at Hampton Beach High*
2. *Showdown at Home Plate*
3. *Outcast on the Court*
4. *Bucky's Big Break*
5. *Bad News in Bangkok*

BAD NEWS IN BANGKOK

David B. Smith

REVIEW AND HERALD® PUBLISHING ASSOCIATION
HAGERSTOWN, MD 21740

The author assumes full responsibility for the accuracy of all facts and quotations as cited in this book.

This book was
Edited by Gerald Wheeler
Designed by Bill Kirstein
Cover art by Scott Snow
Typeset: 11/12 Optima

PRINTED IN U.S.A.

97 96 95 94 93 92 10 9 8 7 6 5 4 3 2 1

R&H Cataloging Service
Smith David B., 1955–
Bad news in Bangkok.

I. Title.

813.54

ISBN 0-8280-0677-6

ONE

SUMMER AT THE BANK

"First California Bank. May I help you?" The words came almost automatically as Bucky continued entering figures into the computer terminal even while answering the phone. He listened to the caller's question. "No, just till noon on Saturdays. Nine to 4:00 all the others."

Bucky made a tiny motion to his customer, as if to apologize for the delay. "Well, the ATM's always open, of course." He briefly described the bank's location, then hung up after saying goodbye.

"You people are busy today," said the short, plump woman who had waited patiently during the call.

The young teller sighed. "Yeah. Lot of calls. Sorry to make you wait like this."

"That's all right." Despite the air-conditioning, she mopped at her perspiring forehead. "Once you take my money, I've got nothing else to do."

The boy grinned as he carefully put her bills into his cash drawer. Initialing the deposit slip, he slid it across to her. "There you are, Mrs. Doherty."

She folded the small piece of paper before putting it away in her huge purse. "Where's that little red-haired girl who usually works here?"

"You mean Sheila?"

"I think that's her name."

"She just had her baby. A little girl. So she's off for a little while."

"Oh, that's nice!" the woman beamed. "Tell her congratulations for me. I'll have to bring her one of my special baby powder sets. I get them half-price at work."

"She'd like that."

A few moments later Bucky glanced up at the wall clock—3:45. Outside it was a hotter-than-usual Bay Area afternoon and without a cloud in the sky. He leaned over the counter to see a little boy standing there. "Hi. Can I help you?"

Taking the child's fistful of dollar bills and coins, he showed him how to add up his deposit.

"What are you saving up for?"

"A bike." The third-grader's eyes shone.

A buzz of conversation over near the front door distracted him. "Sheila!"

The diminutive redhead strutted proudly into the bank, protectively holding her new baby. "Just had to come show off," she announced to the bank employees gathering around her.

Mr. Willis poked his head out of the manager's

office. "Did I hear that our latest dependent has made her debut?"

Sheila beamed. "Here she is. Andrea." She pronounced the name very carefully, with the second, accented syllable rhyming with "tree."

"What a pretty name!" Veronica, the assistant manager, gently ran her finger across the newborn's soft cheek. "Did you pick it out?"

Sheila laughed. "Well, Jeff and I went round and round, and I finally won."

"How was . . . you know, the hospital and everything?" Bucky wanted to know.

The teller made a face. "Twenty hours. Just awful. It went on and on. I swear I thought I'd die." She glanced down at her child. "But soon as Andrea showed up, I didn't mind anymore."

One of First California Bank's regular customers poked his head into the little group of bank employees. "So this is the famous baby we heard all about during that bank robbery a few months ago."

"Yeah." Sheila gave the baby an affectionate kiss. "But thanks to Bucky here, we got through that one, too."

The teenage boy laughed. "Poor kid's been through two pretty tough experiences even before the ink's dry on her birth certificate."

"Yeah, she's a sturdy little thing. To get through that labor, she had to be." Sheila grimaced. "Jeff and I were in there for 17 hours, and I was still only at six centimeters. Doctor began to talk about c-sections, which I for sure didn't want. But all of a sudden, everything began to break loose. Three hours later, this old thing finally showed up."

She shifted the infant in her arms. "Bucky, could

you watch her for just a second? I have to get some things out from the back room."

"Sure." Bucky grinned as he carefully and awkwardly took the baby girl from her. The tiny bundle squirmed in his arms. *Look cool,* he thought to himself. *You're bigger than she is. Don't be afraid of her. She won't break.*

"She's so light," he murmured. A new emotion fluttered through him. *What would it be like to be a father someday?*

"Well, we better get to work again," Mr. Willis observed casually. "Bucky, I guess you know all about banking with one hand. If you can manage with a cast, you can make do with a baby for a couple minutes."

"That's true." The 6-foot-4 boy looked down at the gurgling infant. "Come on, Andrea, let's go wait on some customers."

He nestled the baby in his arms and went back to his teller station, where a gray-haired woman stood patiently. "Can I help you?"

"Well, young man, I need this check cashed. And if you're handing out free babies with every new account, maybe I'll open one. That one sure is a sweetheart."

Bucky laughed. "They used to give out toasters, but they don't even do that anymore." He counted out the bills for his customer.

"Is she yours?"

"Oh, no. I'm still in high school." Turning, he looked around to see if Sheila was coming back yet. "One of our employees just had her last week."

"Here I am." The young mother picked up Andrea and nuzzled her. "Did Bucky treat you all right?" She pretended to listen for a response. "She says you did fine."

The last customer left, leaving him and Sheila alone for a moment. "She's pretty," Bucky murmured.

"Yeah, she's special."

Thoughtfully Bucky slid his cash drawer shut. "You know, Sheila," he began, "I just want you to know . . . I've been praying for you."

The young woman glanced at him.

"I mean, being a mom and everything is sure a big job. But God will help you to do it right. Really."

The redhead's expression sobered. "Yeah." She studied him. "Thanks."

The sun was still high in the sky as he drove home after work. Even at 5:30 the temperature was just beginning to dip down into the low 80s. Bucky flipped on the radio to catch the early innings of the Giants' east coast game with the Expos.

"After one-and-a-half, it's two to nothing, Montreal." Bucky grimaced at the score.

As the sporty white Toyota pulled up at the curb on Woodman Avenue, he saw Rachel Marie dart out of the garage, a big paper sack over her head. She ran up to the passenger side and pressed against the window. "Boo!"

"Hey, Squirt-o," he teased, climbing out of the little car. "Are you trying to scare me?"

"Yep." The 8-year-old came around the car and grabbed onto his leg. "There, I'm not going to let go."

"Help! I've got a tumor!" Bucky staggered up the sidewalk, pretending to shake his little sister loose. "I can't get rid of her."

Rachel Marie squealed with delight as he

clumped into the living room. "Mom! There's a rumor—that I've got a tumor." It was an old Stone family joke.

"A 65-pound tumor?"

"Feels more like 165," Bucky complained with a mock scowl on his face. "A big fat tumor. You better take me in for surgery."

"No!" Rachel Marie released her grasp. "Don't chop me off!"

"We've got a visitor," Mom smiled, motioning her son into the family room.

"Pastor Jensen. Hi!" Bucky pulled his sister to her feet and gave her bottom a healthy swat. "I didn't see your car out front."

"Well, there was a big delivery truck there when I got here, so I parked across the street."

The casually-dressed, silver-haired minister shook hands with Bucky before sitting back down. "How's work?"

"Pretty good." The teenage boy managed a grin. "Full-time days are kind of long sometimes. But the pay's good."

"Yes, that was a real opportunity the Lord gave you." The pastor smiled his thanks as Bucky's mom brought glasses of fruit drink in for them. He took a long sip. "Boy, that's good." Then he drained the glass and set it down. "How's Dan getting along?"

"Good."

"You fellows about halfway through your Bible lessons?"

"Yeah." Bucky pondered. "We're just getting to that stuff on Daniel."

Pastor Jensen nodded, pleased. He reached down and rubbed at a smudge on his shoe before continuing. "Listen, Bucky, I had a call today from a friend of mine. His name's Gordon, and he's just come on here at the conference office. He's helping to coordinate a mission volunteer group here in Northern California."

"What's that?"

"Oh, these teams of young people go out for a couple of weeks and help build a church or mission school in a foreign country. It's a great experience, and the kids who go really have a fantastic time."

Bucky felt a tingle of interest. "Is he planning a trip somewhere?"

The pastor grinned. "Well, that's just it. He's working on one for this August, and he needed an extra name or two. I told him I thought I knew of one."

The youth set down his drink, sitting up straighter. "You're kidding. Me?"

"You got it."

"Where are they going to go?"

Pastor Jensen hesitated for a minute, a mysterious smile on his face. "Well, I'll tell you something. This is the trip of all trips. He's putting a group of kids together to go clear around the world to the Orient. Gordon wants to build a dormitory in northern Thailand."

"Where?"

TWO

MISSION TRIP?

The pastor chuckled. "Yeah, that's what I said when I first heard about it. But I'll tell you, this is the chance of a lifetime, Buck."

Young Stone shook his head. "I just sort of know where Thailand even is. Isn't it by Vietnam and everything?"

"Pretty close. Thailand, Malaysia, Singapore, Kampuchea—what used to be Cambodia—Vietnam. All those countries are near each other."

"Is it safe?"

The older man nodded. "Gordon tells me Thailand and Malaysia have been the two countries in that region to really remain stable for a long, long time. For some reason Communism just never took hold there."

"How long does it take to get there?"

"Oh, it's a looooong plane ride," Pastor Jensen

grinned. "Twenty-some hours. Plus you lose a day going over, then you get it back coming home."

"When are they going?" Bucky was bursting with questions.

"Last two weeks of August. You'd get back just before school started." He hesitated. "You still going to high school this fall?"

"I guess." The teenage boy glanced upstairs to where he knew Dad was working. "Last I heard."

Pastor Jensen studied the tall youth carefully. "If you're interested, why don't we get your folks in here and give them the scoop?" He grinned. "And I get the impression you're interested!"

"Boy, I sure am!" Bucky got to his feet. "Mom?" Going over to the stairway, he climbed up to the first landing. "Dad?"

A minute later the four of them sat in the family room. Mr. Stone shook hands with Pastor Jensen. "Nice to see you again."

"It's good to see you too, Phil." Pastor Jensen, always good with names, remembered easily. Quickly he explained the volunteer mission program to the Stones.

"What's this cost?" Dad gave his son a little punch on the arm.

The pastor looked down at a folder he had pulled from his pocket. "Well, the bottom line is this. Each young person who goes is expected to raise $750. That includes airfare and a round-trip train ticket from Bangkok to a town called Chiang Mai. The academy they're going to is about 30 miles from there." He laughed. "Gordon tells me it's really out in the sticks."

Dad furrowed his brow. "Seven hundred and fifty

bucks? I mean, that's a lot of money, sure. But you can't fly out to the Orient for that."

"You're right," Pastor Jensen hastened. "I guess they've negotiated an exceptional deal with the airline going over, plus the conference is kicking in a little bit to get the program started."

"Are we expected to come up with the $750 ourselves," Mom wanted to know.

"No." The pastor shook his head emphatically. "In fact, that's exactly what we *don't* want. The idea is to raise the money as a church. And, of course, if relatives and people like that want to chip in, that's helpful too."

Bucky thought hard. "What kind of kids go on these trips?"

"That's what I think is so great. They're all super young people, all Adventists." Pastor Jensen caught himself as he glanced over at Mr. Stone. "I mean, it'd give you a chance to meet more guys"—he smiled—"and girls who have some of the same religious background you do, Buck."

The boy mulled over the last statement. The past two years had been hard, with few opportunities to really socialize in a way consistent with his Adventist beliefs. Of course, there was Sam. And now Dan. But meeting good Christian girls had been a near impossibility. A vision of Deirdre with her stunning good looks—and disdainful rejection of Adventism—jolted him back to reality.

"Do these programs always go clear around the world?" he asked.

The minister shook his head. "No, I think this is the first time. The last few years they've usually gone down to places like Honduras or other Central American countries. I guess most of the time they all get together in Miami, Florida, and head out from there. So this is kind of new."

Dad's face was thoughtful. "Are the kids looked after pretty good? I mean, I know Bucky's able to take care of himself. Still . . ."

"Oh, sure. This friend of mine, Gordon—well, Pastor Humboldt—he'll be with them the whole way. And like I said, where they're going is pretty safe territory. We've had a good mission program there for years."

"What exactly would we be doing?" Bucky wondered.

"From what I understand, building a new girls' dormitory at a little academy they run out in the hill country. I'm not sure how to you say it: Mae Dhang." He stumbled over the foreign name.

Mr. Stone scratched his head. "North Thailand. That's opium territory," he observed. "Gangs have run heroin out of there for years."

The pastor nodded. "Gordon tells me that's quite a ways away from where the academy is. Those opium tribes *are* still up there, but I guess they stay located in one little sector and just don't ever come out. Apparently that's not a worry."

"What's it like weather-wise?" Bucky inquired.

"That I don't know. Hot, I'm sure. 'Specially in August. I imagine it'll be shorts and tank tops the whole time."

"Where would we sleep and everything? And eat?"

Pastor Jensen held up both hands in mock surrender. "I give up!" He shook his head. "Sorry I don't know more about this, folks. I imagine they'll just have you stay in one of the other dorms or classrooms or something. Sleeping bags and stuff. And from what I know of those countries, it's probably rice for breakfast, rice for lunch, and rice for dinner. So I hope you like the stuff, Buck."

A shrug. "Sure. I guess."

The man got to his feet. "Well, I really need to let Gordon know by next week, so why don't you talk it over and maybe let me know what you think this Sabbath?"

"That sounds good." Mom came over and gave her son a squeeze. "That's an awful long way from home, Bucky."

"I know, but I want to go." He couldn't hide his excitement.

"Sounds like you've found your man," Dad observed to the pastor.

"I sure hope so. Like I said, let me know." Jensen shook hands with the father and son. "I'll see you later."

Bucky walked with his pastor to the front door.

"And keep up the good work with those Bible studies," the man said before leaving.

* * *

The next evening he and Dan discussed the trip in between Bible verses. "Man, that is one pistol-hot place," the older student grunted. "You sure you want to go packin' way over there?"

"For sure." Bucky leaned back in his chair. "Two weeks? Are you kidding? It's gonna be great."

"I don't know." His stocky friend laughed. "That's a long time away from food made in the good old U.S.A."

"You ought to come, too."

Dan cocked his head, thinking. "Boy, I don't know. Toting concrete blocks out in the jungle?"

"Come on. It'd be great."

Dan was noncommittal. "I'll think about it." Then he laughed. "But not very hard."

Bucky flipped his Bible back open. "Well, at least let's finish this up before it gets dark. I'm gonna squish you at one-on-one."

Carefully the two boys studied the time prophecies in the book of Daniel. Referring to his lesson sheets, Bucky traced the well-known chart showing how the prophetic 2,300 years extended all the way down to 1844.

"Now, look," the younger boy explained. "You start off in 457 B.C. and then run it over until *after* Jesus was born. So you take 483 years and minus 457 from that and it comes right out at 27 A.D."

Dan, scratching with his pencil, scowled at the figures. "More math." He crossed out a number and wrote in another one. "Wait, you heathen. That comes out to 26."

"Huh?" Bucky examined the numbers. "You're right. What'd I do wrong?"

He checked his friend's scrawled numbers again. "I don't get it." He looked down at the bottom of the sheet. "Wait a minute. I remember now. See this note? 'Because there was no zero year between the two eras signified by "B.C." and "A.D." an extra year must be added, bringing the fulfillment of the prophecy to the year 27 A.D.' " He sat back with a satisfied grin. "I remember Pastor Jensen told me that when I studied this, but I guess I forgot about it."

"I don't get it," Dan retorted. "So what's the big

deal if it does come out 27? What's it prove?"

Bucky took a breath. "Well, look." He thought hard. "Here you've got prophecies that happened hundreds of years before Jesus was born. And then it turns out He's baptized in the very year the Bible says the Messiah would be anointed."

Dan considered that. "So?"

"Don't you see? That tells me the Bible's a book I can trust. It's got predictions in it that come true hundreds of years after they were written."

The older student shrugged. "That's OK, I guess. So it worked. Big deal."

"It *is* a big deal," Bucky insisted. "Look. If all these old predictions and promises happened, then where it says Jesus is coming again, *that's* going to take place, too."

Dan chewed on his lip. "Kind of like old what's-his-name in geometry says. If a theorem works a certain number of times, you start to count on it."

"Yeah." Bucky tried to remember an example he'd heard. "Look. Say you're goin' to Candlestick Park for a game but you've never been there before."

"OK."

"So I give you directions: Take the 80 Interstate past the 5 junction, stay on it until you hit the Bay Bridge, cross it, pass the Market Street exit on your right, keep going until you get to the South Bay area, then two miles before the airport you take the second exit for the stadium."

The stocky athlete grinned. "Coming from someone who knows."

"Right. Anyway, so you start out, and as you go along, every landmark is there just like I told you. The Bay Bridge, Market Street, and right down the line.

After a while you say, 'Man, Stone knows what he's talkin' about. I guess I can relax. I'm gonna make it to the game.' "

"Yeah."

"Bible prophecy is like that. The ones that have already worked tell you the rest are going to happen too."

Dan nodded.

"Plus," the younger student added, "all these prophecies tell me that Jesus really was the promised Messiah. He came right on schedule. Look at this chart. He showed up and was baptized *and* crucified exactly when Daniel said he would be. Except that the prophet said it hundreds of years earlier."

An expression of slight amusement on his face, Dan looked at his friend. "You really get into this stuff, don't you?"

Bucky grinned, toying with his pencil. "Well, when something works out as . . . tight as this does, yeah, it makes me feel good about trusting God. I'll admit it."

Dan scribbled down the final answer on his paper. "All right, Rev," he teased. "You've sold me. Now, come on, let's shoot some hoops. We've got a varsity team to make."

The taller boy stretched himself to his full six-foot-four height. "All right!"

The two drove themselves for a hard half hour. Despite a very slight soreness in his still recovering arm, Bucky's skill around the basket had only faded a little bit. "Not bad!" Dan grunted, as Bucky whirled past him for an easy four-foot jump shot.

Bucky plucked the ball out of the air on its way through the net and flipped it to Dan. "You really think we can make varsity this fall?"

"I dunno. Hope so." Dan dribbled to the edge of the driveway and sighted for a long one. The ball teetered on the rim before falling off to the right. The older boy growled in exasperation.

"If you'd grow about two more inches, you'd have a shot at varsity center," he told Bucky. "'Cept I think you've about stopped, haven't you?"

"Yeah." Bucky sighed. "Six-four. That's about it." He tossed the ball over into the grass and sank down to rest on the lawn where he looked up at Dan. "You think we'll have much problem with Friday night games again?"

Dan shook his head. "Boy. Can you imagine what old Brayshaw'll say when he finds out he's got two of us to worry about?" His facial expression tightened. "He's gonna wish he'd never heard about the Sabbath."

"We'll just have to find the right way to tell him," Bucky said slowly. "And then he's got to find a way to make it work."

* * *

The air-conditioned interior of the mall felt good as Bucky and Rachel Marie walked from store to store the next evening. "Aren't you about done with your ice cream?" he asked.

"Uh huh." She took one last bite and wiped her chubby hands on her pink pants. "Thank you, Bucky."

"You're welcome." He gave his little sister a grin. "My treat."

She reached up and took his hand. The sticky remains of the cone clung to his skin. "What are we going to get for Mommy?"

"Well, you're supposed to be looking," he reminded. "Shall we go in there?"

The pair walked into the Woolworth discount store to find an inexpensive birthday gift.

"I like these!" Rachel Marie exclaimed, heading toward a long rack of teddy bears.

"Silly, we're buying something Mommy would like, not you."

"She'd like these," the little girl protested.

"No way. Come on, help me find something she'd like."

"Well, Mr. Stone," a husky voice purred behind him. "And Miss Stone."

Bucky didn't need to even turn around. "Deirdre!"

The blonde batted her eyelashes at him with her trademark smile. "So this is your new woman?"

"Yeah. My sister Rachel Marie." He coughed nervously. "This is Deirdre. Remember from last year?"

"Uh huh." Bucky's sister was unimpressed. "Come on, Bucky."

The teenage boy gave Deirdre a resigned look. "Shopping for my mom," he murmured.

"That's nice." She gave her short skirt a tug. "What have you been up to?"

Bucky's pulse was still racing unevenly. *Deirdre was too gorgeous to pass up!* He thought back to the previous school year's painful romance. "Oh, not much," he replied lamely. "Still working at the bank. Oh, I might be going over to the Orient in August."

"Wow! Really?"

"Yeah. It's a church-building trip." The comment tumbled out before he could catch himself.

At the mention of church, the blonde's coolness returned. "So you're off to mission lands, huh? I thought maybe you were just going sightseeing."

Rachel Marie tugged at his hand again. "Yeah, well, it's kind of a neat thing. Actually, 'bout 15 kids going to Thailand to help this school build a dormitory." He began to follow his little sister toward the back of the store.

"Have fun." Deirdre's voice was even.

As his sister tugged him out of her sight, he glanced back at the slim girl.

THREE

PERMISSION TO BE BAPTIZED

The last notes of the quartet faded away in the Sabbath twilight. The people in the half-filled church murmured enthusiastic "Amen"s as three of the members sat down.

Mr. Sawyer, the big bass, remained by the microphone for just a minute. "I just want to encourage all of you here to give a good gift for Bucky's trip," he added. "When he goes out to the Orient to help build that dormitory, he'll be doing it for all of us. This is *our* mission project, and I know this experience will be a real blessing for him."

Pastor Jensen walked up to the platform and shook hands with the singer. "Thanks, Ralph. And thanks to all our musicians who helped make our musical program a success. Especially those of you from our neighbor churches. That was some great music, and we all enjoyed it."

The congregation clapped heartily before he went on. "These last few years I've seen a real missionary spirit in Bucky Stone. Going to high school here, he's been a great witness for God. He helped bring Sam into our church family, and I understand we may have another baptism before too many weeks go by.

"But now, let's give Bucky a chance at some real mission experience with young people of his own faith," the pastor urged. "These two weeks will be a time he'll never forget as he works side by side with fellow Adventist young people to build that dormitory for those students there in Thailand. I want Bucky to come up right now and just say a word telling us how he feels about all this."

Slowly Bucky made his way up to the platform where he stood next to the pastor. "Go ahead, Bucky," Pastor Jensen urged. "Just share your thoughts with us."

The boy took a deep breath. "Well, I . . . I just think it would be great to try, you know, being a missionary for two weeks. It's a really neat project, building a dorm for the kids over there, and I think it'll give me a real picture of what mission life is like." He looked out at the attentive faces of his church family before continuing.

"And I, well . . . I guess to be with a bunch of kids who are all Adventists . . ." He left the thought unfinished as a quiet ripple of assent filled his ears.

Pastor Jensen put an arm around the young man. "Now we've handed out envelopes for each of you to use. And I want to say again, everything we give toward this trip is mission money for *all* of us. Bucky represents the Hampton Beach Adventist Church over there in Thailand. And I know God is going to use him."

Twenty minutes later Bucky and Mom sat with the pastor in his office counting up the pledges. "Look at this," Pastor Jensen commented. "Fifty dollars from old Mrs. Cordell. Bless her heart."

"And here's one with just two quarters in it." Bucky looked at the childish scrawl on the envelope. "From Sissy."

"Oh, you know who that is," the pastor smiled. "That little Black girl who always sits right there on the front row."

"That's so sweet." Mom held the two quarters for a moment, her eyes thoughtful.

Jensen punched in the final figures. "Well, Bucky, you're on your way. Sort of," he added. "Four hundred fifty-five dollars. And 50 cents." He nodded toward the two quarters with a grin.

"Well, I've still got a good share of the summer to come up with the rest," Bucky observed.

"You'll make it." The smiling pastor clapped him on the shoulder.

* * *

Wednesday evening Bucky sat in the leather seat of Dan's sports car. "Boy, I hope this goes OK," he muttered to his friend.

"You and me both." Dan squinted as the setting sun glared in his rear view mirror. With a squeal of the tires, he pulled up at the familiar house.

"Is he home?"

"Yeah." Dan glanced at his watch. "Told me he was going to be in tonight. 'Stead of at the bar like usual."

The two made their way up to the front door. Easing it open, Dan gave Bucky a friendly little push. "After you, man."

"That you?" Coming from the back of the house, the words had a slur to them.

"Yeah, Dad. I'm home." Dan paused. "I got Bucky here with me."

"Oh. Sure." There was a loud cough. "Be right out."

Bucky glanced around the living room. It was cleaner than last winter, he noticed, when he had driven Dan home that painful afternoon the boy had come to basketball practice drunk.

Dan glanced sideways at his friend. "You thinkin' about the same thing I am?" he muttered with a crooked grin.

Bucky shrugged. "Long time ago."

A skinny man in his late 40s came out of the shadows, dressed in a pair of jeans and undershirt. His stubble looked about two days old.

"This your friend?"

"Yeah. Dad, this is Bucky Stone."

Mr. Litton wiped his hands on his greasy jeans and moved warily toward Bucky. "How are you?" He offered his hand.

"Good."

The three of them stood awkwardly in the shadows of the dingy living room. "Well, look, have a seat, Bucky." The older man pushed aside some newspapers and sat down on an old piano bench. "Dan, here, tells me you boys both want to talk to me. Something important, he says."

Bucky licked his lips. "Yeah. Well . . ." He paused. "*You* tell him."

Dan cleared his throat nervously, giving his friend

a pained expression. "I . . . I guess you're right."

"Come on, come on." Mr. Litton's words were impatient. "What's the matter with you guys? Out with it."

"Well . . . yeah. It's like this." Dan's normally cocky manner was almost timid. He traced a design in the dirty carpet with his foot. "I've been goin' to church with Bucky, here, for a pretty long time, and I've decided to join. So I decided to ask you."

The older man sat with a blank look on his face. "That's it?"

His response took Dan by surprise. "Yeah. I guess." He forced a laugh.

"So join. I don't care." Mr. Litton flicked some grease off his thumbnail. "I guess goin' to church won't do you any harm."

"Great! Well, I guess that's it." Pleased, Dan looked over at his classmate.

"What kind of church is it?" his father asked innocently.

Dan scratched at his short athletic haircut. "It's the Seventh-day Adventist Church." He gave Bucky another sidelong glance. "We've been goin' there quite a while. I really like it a lot."

"Wait a minute." Mr. Litton sat up a little straighter. "What'd you call it?"

Bucky cleared his throat. "It's the Seventh-day Adventist Church here in town. I . . . I've been going there for several years, and Dan started coming with me a while back."

"What kind of thing is that?" All of a sudden the questions had a little edge to them.

"Well . . . I don't know what you want to know. They go to church on Saturday instead of Sunday.

Except for that, it's pretty much like what we went to when . . . Mom lived with us."

"Saturday!"

Dan's face reddened a little bit. "Dad, I've been going there Saturdays for months. You knew I was going. What's the big deal now?"

Mr. Litton glanced from one boy to the other. "I don't . . . I guess I wasn't thinking much about it." Abruptly he went into the kitchen. From his chair Bucky could see him peering into the refrigerator. The older man muttered a short oath to himself. A moment later he reached into the cupboard. The two boys could hear the splash of liquid.

Bucky gave Dan a nervous look. "What do you think?" he mouthed noiselessly. His friend gave him a quieting gesture.

The father returned to the living room with a tumbler of amber liquid in his hand. Before speaking he took a long swallow. "Look," he said, directing his remarks toward Bucky. "You bein' friends with Dan, here, that's fine. I guess you two do pretty good at ball and everything." Another swallow. "But this business of church and Saturday and everything . . ." The words trailed off while he drained the glass. "No way."

"But, Dad . . ."

"No!" Mr. Litton scowled at his son. "I was brought up a Baptist, and even if I don't go to church much right now, I know one thing's for sure. And that's that this Saturday stuff's dead wrong."

"Dad . . ."

"You listen to me! I know something about you people." The man pointed an unsteady finger in Bucky's face. "That Saturday stuff . . . and business about keeping all them old Jewish laws and not eating any meat and everything." He wiped at his mouth with his soiled sleeve. "You just leave me and my boy out of it!"

"You've got it all wrong." Dan's voice tensed up a little bit. "This church isn't like that."

"And I'm sayin' it is!"

Slowly Bucky rose to his feet. "Listen," he said softly, "why don't we talk about it some other time." He took a deep breath. "Mr. Litton, if you'd like, I'd be happy for my pastor to come over and answer any questions you have about our church."

"I don't have any questions. See?" The words were clipped, sarcastic.

The boy flushed. "I think it's good for you to be interested in what your son chooses," he said evenly. "I mean . . . that shows you care."

The quiet words had an effect. "Yeah, well, I just don't want him getting mixed up in some nutball group." Mr. Litton snorted. "No offense."

Bucky looked at his friend. "Can you give me a ride home?"

"Sure." Dan's face was a deep red. "Come on."

The two boys headed toward the front door. "It was nice to meet you," Bucky offered as they exited.

The older man said nothing, just stood in the doorway with a dour expression on his face.

"Well, that was cheerful," Dan stormed as the car's powerful engine eased them out of the driveway.

Bucky forced a laugh. "For a second I thought we were home free. Then everything hit the fan."

The stocky driver snorted. "You're so stinking friendly to everybody. 'Thank you, Mr. Litton, for kicking my tail in.'" He mimicked Bucky with sarcastic accuracy.

Both boys laughed. "Hey, there ain't no sense in making him mad," Bucky observed. "One way or another, we've got to win your dad over."

Dan sobered. "Yeah."

The next day at the bank Mr. Litton's words kept ringing in the young teller's ears. "Nutball group. Nutball group." During a break he breathed a quick prayer, asking God to help him demonstrate the thoughtful wisdom of Adventism to Dan's father.

"How's the trip coming?" Mr. Willis came up behind Bucky with a broad smile.

"Well, I'm getting pretty excited." Bucky handed over two $20 bills to a customer. "I really appreciate you giving me the two weeks off."

"Oh, no problem." The manager's neatly tailored coat gave him a dignified look that didn't quite mask his cheerful nature. "Is the fundraising coming all right?"

The young man frowned slightly. "Well, the church raised about $450. Then some of my relatives helped out with about a hundred bucks. I'm shy about $200, I guess."

"Boy, that's no good." Mr. Willis's brow furrowed. "And you've only got about three weeks left." The manager thought a moment. "Well," he said at last, "I don't want you to be all worried and bothered about that money and scowling at the customers and everything."

"Oh, I won't." What was he getting at?

Trying to mask his broad grin, Mr. Willis pulled a long white envelope out of his pocket. "Maybe this will help keep you a cheerful smiling employee of First California Bank."

His pulse tingling, Bucky tore the envelope open. "What?"

There in his hand was a check made out for exactly $200.

Bucky's voice had a note of awe in it. "How'd you know?"

"I didn't." Mr. Willis smiled. "But I guess God knew that's how much you needed."

The student teller cleared his throat. "Mr. Willis, I . . . sure appreciate this, but is it really OK for the bank to . . ." His voice failed him.

The man put a hand on the teenage boy's shoulder. "Bucky, this is from me."

Bucky glanced down at the check. Sure enough, the manager's home address appeared in the upper-left corner.

"When you started working here, I told you my mother was an Adventist," the older man said softly. "In a way, I guess I want to do this in honor of her. To have you going on this trip for your church . . . well, I just wanted to help."

"Wow." There wasn't much else to say.

"And, of course, you know what I think of you."

Taking a deep breath, Bucky nodded and stuck out his hand. "Thanks a lot, Mr. Willis. This really means a lot to me."

The hand on his shoulder tightened. "Just make sure you come back after those two weeks are done. This bank isn't about to let you get away, and last time I checked, First California didn't have any branch offices in Bangkok!"

* * *

The next three weeks flew by in a flurry of activity as Bucky read brochures, received his passport in the mail, and began counting down the days.

"One more week!" he grinned at Dan as the pair wrapped up their final Bible study.

"Yeah, I'll be glad when you get out of here and leave me alone." Dan pretended to scowl. "Zooming through these studies like this—man, this has been harder than Test Week."

"Hey, you said you wanted to finish before I left."

Dan filled in the final blank on the youth Bible lessons and slid the paper toward his friend. "I gotta admit, you were dead right on all this stuff. It makes sense."

"Yeah." A moment of thoughtful silence. "You know, I think *that's* what I want more than anything to tell people. That this stuff *makes sense*. It's just . . . right."

Dan grinned at him, then quickly sobered. "What are we gonna do about my dad?"

Bucky didn't answer. It was a question that had nagged him ever since the unpleasant visit several weeks earlier.

"I mean, do I just go ahead and get baptized without saying nothin'?"

His friend shook his head. "No way. At least, I think we've got to try talking to him again."

"Oh, man." Dan grimaced. "You heard what he said."

"Yeah, but look." Bucky grappled to find the right words. "He's upset because he thinks things are a certain way. But they're not. That's the whole point. Being a Christian—and an Adventist—isn't what he thinks it is. We just gotta find a way to tell him that."

"Good luck." Dan examined a long scar on his ankle. "I got another happy challenge for you. What's old Brayshaw going to do when he finds out he's got two Adventists on his basketball team now?"

Bucky began to laugh. "He'll just have to call the district office and tell 'em, 'From now on the Panthers play triple headers every Thursday night.' "

That Friday evening it was a reluctant pair of boys who followed Pastor Jensen up the driveway to Dan's home. "I hope you got a bulletproof vest on," Dan said to the pastor, his voice tight with apprehension.

"Relax." The older man clapped him on the back. "I've been through things like this more times than I can count."

Mr. Litton scowled when he saw the visitor, but motioned the three into the dismal living room. "I told Dan he was barkin' up the wrong tree, but doesn't seem like he's in a mood to listen to me," he told Jensen without fanfare.

"Well, I'm just here to see if I can help clear things up," the pastor said easily. "Why don't we just all have a seat and chat for a bit?"

The two boys sat down on the couch and looked from one man to the other. "What kind of work are you in, Mr. Litton?" Jensen began.

Dan's father chewed on his lip. "Auto service. Over at Sears."

"Oh really? I've had work done over there before. We'll have to look for you next time."

Mr. Litton studiously disdained the friendly overture.

The pastor took a breath. "Boy, a lot of that computer diagnostic stuff you guys have now—that's pretty complicated stuff."

"Yeah, well, after 15 years, you get the hang of it."

Pastor Jensen glanced over at the boys. "Dan tells

me you sort of have a background in the Baptist religion."

Mr. Litton cleared his throat. "Yeah, well, I guess. We haven't gone for a while, but that's how I was raised."

"I have a lot of good friends who are Baptists," the pastor smiled. "In fact, I was at a Bible conference last spring, and I roomed with a terrific young man who pastors a Baptist church up in Oregon. We had a wonderful time together."

The dark-haired man showed the first spark of interest. "I always kind of figured you folks stuck to yourselves. With Saturday and everything."

"Oh, my, no." Pastor Jensen shook his head vigorously. "I belong to the Pastors' Council here in town, and we have a great time worshiping with each other. Every two months we have a big breakfast together and talk about our common problems." He laughed. "I guess offerings are down in just about every church!"

His efforts were lost on the dour man. "Look, what's your point? Come on."

Pastor Jensen leaned forward. "Well, I want you to know that I certainly understand how you feel. At the same time, I want you to know that Adventists and Baptists have a great deal in common."

"Oh yeah?"

"Absolutely. In fact, on virtually all the main points of Christianity, Adventists and Baptists hold almost identical views. Jesus dying on the cross for our sins, Creation, the Trinity—you know, God the Father, Son, and Holy Ghost—and just a whole lot more." He counted them off on his fingers. "Trusting in God for salvation. Believing that the Bible is God's

Word. In fact, Adventists often say that a great portion of their belief system is a heritage from the Baptist faith. My old seminary professor used to say that all the time."

"Yeah, Dad." Bucky looked up in surprise as Dan interjected a comment. "It's really just about the same as what I always heard before. Except for going to church on Saturday instead of Sunday."

"Oh, there's other stuff too," his father retorted. "What about when people die, and what happens then? Somebody at work told me your bunch is way out on a limb on that."

Pastor Jensen grinned and held up both hands. "Mr. Litton, I've got to hand it to you. You're a man who thinks and has opinions. I like that."

The younger man grunted, his eyes brooding.

"Well, look. We sure won't solve some of these things just in one evening here. But the point is, Dan has studied pretty carefully for months now, and from what he's learned, he thinks the Adventist Church is where he'd like to be. We're just here to see if you object."

"He knows I object. There ain't no debate on it." Bucky looked over at Dan.

Pastor Jensen nodded slowly. "Well, I appreciate your honesty. You've been real open with me about your feelings, and that helps." He took a breath. "And frankly, if you don't approve, well, then Dan just won't be baptized."

"What?" Dan shifted in his seat, staring at the minister with resentment in his dark eyes.

"Dan, you know how eager I am to have you join the church," Pastor Jensen said softly. "But you're still living here at home, and you owe your dad some loyalty. If he tells you not to be baptized right now, I feel that you should obey him."

Even Bucky was confused. "But look . . ."

"Look, fellows." The pastor shifted in his seat and turned toward them. "Here's how I look at it. When Dan turns 18, then he has an absolute right to join any church he wants to. I'm sure even your dad here, Dan, would see it that way. I mean, that kind of freedom's what America's all about. And even before then, Mr. Litton, I hope you'll let Dan come to our church each week if he think's it's helping him."

Mr. Litton scowled, looking at the pastor suspiciously.

"But as long as you're living here, Dan, at least until you turn 18 . . . I think you ought to respect your dad's wishes."

The son appeared about to reply, but he held his silence. At last he gave a big sigh. "Yeah, OK." He looked up at his father. "Whatever you want, Dad. That's fine, I guess."

"But now let me say this, too." The older man turned back toward Mr. Litton. "As clear as I can see it, being around Bucky has really helped your son. Last year with some of the problems and all . . ." He carefully avoided mentioning Dan's drinking.

The father shrugged. "Yeah. I'll grant you that. So?"

"I hope you'll keep this in mind. It's Bucky's faith in God—and now Dan's faith in God as well—that has made them the solid young men they're becoming." He looked over at the two. "I mean, these two fellows have got their act together, and everybody over at that high school knows it. And it's their religion that has made 'em that way."

Mr. Litton gave a noncommittal shrug.

The pastor rose to depart. "I really hope that when the time comes when Dan is able to make his decision, that you'll be able to stand with him and support him on it." His voice was gentle. "I've baptized a few people whose relatives were upset. You know? Angry . . . and they'd stay away. And that's a tough thing for someone to go through, especially a young person."

Reaching toward Litton, he offered a handshake. "When Dan's moment comes, I just want you to know, we'd be real proud to have you sitting there on the front row letting him know that you're a dad who cares."

Mr. Litton accepted the pastor's hand and gave a tiny nod, his eyes deep in thought. "Yeah. Well . . ." His gaze jerked from the pastor to his son and Bucky. Dan, who had been sitting quietly with his head in his hands, met his father's gaze.

FOUR

TRAFFIC JAM ON THE BAY BRIDGE

". . . And lead us not into temptation, but deliver us from evil." Next to him, Bucky could hear Rachel Marie's soft 8-year-old voice. She knew the Lord's Prayer as well as any adult. Risking a peek, he glanced down at his little sister as she recited it.

"For thine is the kingdom and the power and the glory forever. Amen." Bucky's bass voice joined with Sam's as the congregational prayer concluded. The row of worshipers resumed their seats and looked expectantly toward the platform.

Black-robed Pastor Jensen waded gingerly into the filled baptistery. "This is the moment we've been waiting for," he beamed. "Dan, come on in."

Bucky's heart skipped a beat as he watched his friend slowly lower himself into the tank of water.

"And we have some people in the congregation I want to invite to come forward," the minister continued. "Sam, I want you up here. Bucky, you too. In fact, all of you Stones might as well join us."

Startled, Mom and Rachel Marie went up with Bucky to stand near the baptistery. Bucky gave his friend a thumbs-up gesture.

"Twice now we've had baptisms in this church as a result of Bucky's willingness to share his faith," Pastor Jensen observed as he stood waist-deep in the water. "But I know how Mrs. Stone has had Sam and now Dan over to her home, and made them feel welcome. In fact, Jen, it's probably your cooking as much as anything that has brought these fine young men into God's family!" Everyone in the building chuckled.

"And we have a very special guest here this morning," the pastor added. "Dan's father, Mr. Litton, is here today, and we're so glad that Dan has his support. Mr. Litton, why don't you come up front too? We're delighted that you're our visitor today and just want you to feel welcome."

Dan's father blinked once, then stood with the rest. Dan, also robed in black, looked up at his father.

Bucky felt his stomach do a flip-flop as he watched the unexpected scene. It had been just that morning that Mr. Litton had abruptly made up his mind to attend the service.

"Dan," Pastor Jensen began, "you have a good earthly father here. And a heavenly Father who loves you just as much. I know how faithfully you've studied the Bible, trying to discover just what kind of God we serve. And now that you've found Jesus to be a true Friend, you've chosen to give your heart to Him."

The quiet hum of the air conditioning in the background seemed to add to the peacefulness that filled the sanctuary.

"And now in this public setting, Dan, you're saying to your family, to your friends, to your high school classmates: 'I choose God. I want to faithfully serve Him.' And I want you to know that this church family stands right with you, praying for you as you witness for Him." The baptismal candidate nodded.

"And so, Dan, because you love Jesus, it's my great joy today to baptize you in the name of the Father, the Son, and the Holy Spirit. Amen."

Bucky glanced at Sam with a smile as the quiet ceremony concluded. Mr. Litton watched without comment.

It was 20 minutes past noon before the large throng of believers spilled out into the foyer and front lawn of the SDA church. A rare August drizzle went almost unnoticed. Dan, his hair nearly dry, accepted the good wishes of the members as they filed by.

"Can you stay for lunch today?" Pastor Jensen gave the new church member an enthusiastic welcome handshake. "Your dad, too, of course."

Litton glanced over at his father. "Well, I think Dad wants to get going."

"How about you?"

The young man shook his head. "I'm going with him."

The pastor gave a nod of understanding. "That's good," he affirmed. He reached over and offered his hand to Mr. Litton. "Thanks so much for coming. It was a treat to have you here."

"Yeah." The middle-aged man looked around at the flow of worshipers. "Lot of people."

"It's a pretty terrific bunch." Pastor Jensen waved to one family just climbing into their station wagon. "I hope you can come again some time."

"We'll see." Mr. Litton motioned toward his son. "Ready?"

"Sure." Dan gave Bucky a grin of relief. "All set for tomorrow?"

"Yup. You won't forget?"

"Nine o'clock. Get you to the airport by 11:00 easy."

"Tomorrow's the big day?" Mrs. Jensen clutched her husband's arm as he continued to greet visitors.

"Yeah!" Bucky couldn't hide his excitement. "Thailand, here I come!"

"I'm jealous," she laughed. "Bring me back a souvenir. Some of that Thai silk."

* * *

The next morning arrived with a splash. The 10:00 p.m. weather forecast the night before had predicted more drizzle, but Hampton Beach seemed to be the center of a full-force storm. Bucky looked out the window at the gloom.

"You boys better plan an extra half-hour to get to the airport," Mom observed as she plopped a third helping of French toast onto his plate.

"I know," her tall son muttered as he glanced at his watch. "Soon as I eat these, I'll give Dan a call."

The front doorbell chimed and Dan poked his head through the doorway. "Airport Limo Service," he grinned.

"Man, you're early."

"Hey," Dan retorted, "in this slop it's going to take us a lot longer. Plus we gotta pick Sam up."

"Well, eat some of this French toast for me, and then we'll go."

"I won't make you beg me." Dan plopped down with a cheerful grunt. "This looks good!"

"Here you are." Mrs. Stone set a plate of food in front of him.

"Pretty good timing," Bucky teased. "Always around mealtime."

"Shhhhh." Bucky's mother gave him a playful flick on the top of his head. "You're welcome anytime, Dan, and you know it."

Minutes later Bucky lugged his suitcase and duffel bag down the stairs. "Heavy sucker," he complained.

"I read that brochure," his friend teased. "Supposed to bring only three changes of clothes and just keep rotating 'em. You got the whole department store here."

"I know." Bucky paused at the front door. "Well, guess this is it."

Mrs. Stone gave him a big hug. "Honey, I'm going to miss you."

At that moment he realized how far away Thailand's 9,000 miles were going to seem for the next two weeks. "Me, too, Mom." He clung to her for a moment.

"'Bye, Bucky." Rachel Marie tugged on his arm.

He swooped his little sister into his embrace. She squeezed him around the neck. "I love you."

"I love you, too, kid." He gave her a kiss. "You want me to bring you anything from Thailand?"

"I don't know. What do they have?"

"I don't know either. But I'll look, OK?"

Bucky looked at his father. "Goodbye, Dad." He stuck out his hand.

"Hey, cut that out. You're going a long way from home. Give your old man a hug."

"I know. I was only kidding." The two of them embraced. "I'll miss you."

"Take good care of yourself." Mr. Stone looked over at Dan. "I appreciate you guys driving Bucky over to the airport. With this meeting I got this afternoon, I just couldn't have gotten back in time. And I don't want Jenny out in this rain."

"No sweat." Dan picked up Bucky's suitcase with a grunt. "Come on, missionary boy. All those Thai girls are waiting for you."

Bucky watched as the house on Woodman Avenue disappeared around the corner. "Boy, two weeks."

"Piece of cake, Buck, ole man. You'll be back before you know it."

The ride to San Francisco went quickly despite the rain. The freeways were nearly empty as the three of them motored through the downpour.

"You takin' chem this fall?" Sam squinted through the streaked windshield.

Dan grimaced as he changed lanes. "Yeah, me and Stone both, I guess. Sick!"

"I'll loan you all my lab notes. 'Course, most of my experiments never came out like the manual said they were supposed to."

"Thanks a lot." Bucky glanced at his watch. "Man, we're making good time. I'll end up sitting in the terminal for an hour and a half."

"Hey, don't kid yourself." Dan growled something inaudible to himself as he braked. "Taillights coming up."

Bucky frowned as he stared ahead through the

rain. "Oh, brother. What happened?"

"I'll bet somebody slid out on the bridge or something."

Moments later traffic came to a dead stop. "Good thing we've got some extra time," Bucky commented.

The next hour was a slippery stop-and-go experience. Even while bantering with his two friends, Bucky kept glancing at his watch as his reserve of "extra time" disappeared.

"I don't know, Stone," Sam grimaced. "I hope you don't have your heart that set on getting to Bangkok on time."

"Well, with this rain the airlines will probably be running a little late anyway, don't you think?"

"I doubt it. Didn't you say this just takes you up to Portland and then you and the other kids fly out from there?"

"Yeah."

"Well, then, they're not gonna run late on a short hop like Frisco-Portland. Otherwise, that screws up the whole rest of their schedule."

"You're so smart." Bucky's pulse quickened. *"Come on!"*

"You heard much from Lisa lately?" Sam tried to change the subject.

"Yeah, I called her about a week ago."

"You tell her you're going out to the Orient?"

"Yeah." Bucky watched the road signs as they crawled by. At last they passed the main source of trouble: a huge trailer rig blocking two lanes.

"Thanks a lot, sucker!" Dan gave the stranded rig a "raspberry" jeer as the sports car slipped past. "Now we can make some time!"

"Well, let's cruise!" Bucky sucked in his breath as

he glanced down at his watch. "Plane leaves in 20 minutes!"

"Look," Dan said, "we'll just drop you off right there at the curb. You run in and go straight to the gate. Forget check-in. I think you'll just make it."

"What about my suitcase and everything?"

"Forget it! No time. You just carry it on with you. Check it in for good when you get to Portland." Dan gunned the engine and the car shot into the fast lane. "We'll just wait there at the curb for about 15 minutes. If you don't come back out weeping like a baby, we'll know you made it."

Moments later Dan squealed onto the exit ramp marked "Departing Flights."

"Easy!" Despite his nervousness, Bucky managed a short laugh. "I'd like to live to play ball with you this fall!"

"Hey, we're here, man." The stocky driver spotted an opening right next to Delta Airlines' main terminal. "Grab your suitcase and run!"

Sam slid forward so that Bucky could ease through the small opening from the back seat. Dashing to the back of the car he pulled his suitcase and duffel bag free.

"OK, I'm out of here!" Breathing hard, he set the suitcase down for a moment and shook hands with Sam. "Thanks, you guys. I really appreciate it."

"Forget that! Just go!" Dan grinned, reaching out to shake hands, too, and then gave Bucky a forceful wave of dismissal. "Have a good one. We'll see you in a couple of weeks."

Grabbing his suitcase, Bucky jogged toward the front door of the terminal, turning one final time to wave to his two friends.

"Now which gate?" Pausing in front of a TV monitor he spotted the flight number. Moving quickly up the escalator he winced as he saw the long lines just outside security.

"Come on, come on!" he muttered to himself as passengers and bags slowly snaked through the elaborate system. Picking up his suitcase on the other side he jogged down the corridor to the far end.

"Can I still make it?" he panted to the attendant standing at the gate.

The young woman shook her head. "I think they just closed the door."

Bucky groaned. "I can't miss the flight!"

She took his ticket. "We have another one leaving at three."

"But I'm connecting with a group going out to Thailand!"

"Oh, dear. That is bad." She glanced quickly at the ticket, then picked up the phone. "Jim, is the door closed?" She listened for a moment, then set it down. "Go! Quick! They'll let you on." She tore the ticket stub loose and handed the folder back to him.

Heaving a huge sigh of relief, he picked up his bag and trotted down the boarding ramp.

"She's got my ticket," he told the attendant at the end.

"Yeah, I saw her take it. You got lucky, young man."

"I know." With a relieved grin he entered the crowded aircraft.

A stewardess at the door sized him up. "I take it you're the last one. Let me take that suitcase for you. We'll stow it up here."

"Thanks." His heart still beating rapidly, he made

his way to his assigned seat just as the captain's final announcements began.

* * *

Ninety minutes later the Delta airliner touched down in Portland. Bucky looked out the window at the unfamiliar greenery of the Pacific Northwest. "Well, at least I know I'm going to make it," he muttered to himself as he unbuckled his seatbelt. The close call back in San Francisco still had him slightly unnerved.

Out in the main terminal he looked again for the always-present TV monitors listing overseas flights. "Seoul-Taipei-Bangkok. There it is!" He eyed the overhead signs and resolutely headed down the corridor.

In front of Gate 12 milled a group of fresh-faced teenagers. With a confident grin, Bucky headed toward them.

"Are you Bucky Stone?" An athletic-looking man about 40 offered his hand.

"Yep."

"Oh, good! I'm Gordon Humboldt. We were afraid with that storm down your way you wouldn't make it. I was about to go over to the gate where you were coming in, but I figured you'd know how to find us."

"No problem." Bucky grinned. "I made the flight with about two seconds to spare."

"As long as you're here." The cheerful youth leader turned to the others. "You guys, this is Bucky Stone. From . . . where do you live again, Bucky?"

"Hampton Beach. It's real close to San Francisco."

Everybody crowded around to greet him. The

group of 18 appeared to be an even mix of male and female.

"This your first time?" A tall Black student shook hands with Bucky.

"Yeah. How 'bout you?"

"No way! Third time, man. These things are a trip."

Pastor Humboldt gave the tall student a gentle punch on the biceps. "Yeah, Benny, here, is a real regular. If I get Asian flu, I'll just let him run things."

"All right!" Benny's laugh was deep and sincere.

Pastor Humboldt pulled a list out of his pocket and silently scanned it. A moment later he tucked it away and whistled for attention.

"Folks, we're all here now, so let's just gather around for a second before we board."

Bucky glanced around the terminal. Busy travelers scurried toward the various gates and the huge planes bound for overseas destinations. But already he felt that a spirit of togetherness had developed among the 18 students headed for Thailand. A thoughtful smile tugged at the corner of his lips. *This was a family!*

"You heard them say we're being routed through Alaska because of the headwinds," the leader announced. Bucky's eyes opened wide. "So we'll be getting into Bangkok about one in the morning. Let's just take it real easy on this flight. Get all the rest you can, drink plenty of liquid, and the jet lag shouldn't be too bad when we get there."

"Pastor Humboldt? How long is the flight?"

A broad smile. "Well, now, let's ease up on one thing right away. Just to save energy, why don't we all agree that for the next two weeks, you all call me Gordon? OK?"

The girl smiled.

"Anyway, we're in the air a good 20 hours. But it's a big plane, and you can move around all you want." He glanced at his watch. "They'll be announcing it any minute, so let's gather around and have a prayer first."

The enthusiastic group joined hands as Gordon led them in a brief session of prayer. "Lord, help us to do more than just build a dormitory," he entreated. "Anybody could do that. But help us to share with these precious people our love for You—our belief that even though we come from different countries and cultures, we're all brothers and sisters in You."

"Amen." The students murmured the closing together.

"That's us!" The staccato announcement began just as the prayer finished. "Grab your carry-ons, and let's get in line."

Bucky gasped. "My suitcase!" He went up to the leader. "I got on in San Francisco in such a hurry I couldn't check my suitcase. What should I do?"

"Oh, I think they can check it through from this gate here," the leader shrugged. "We got plenty of time. Let's see."

Ten minutes later the student group walked aboard the huge DC-10 with its endless rows of seats. Only the gentle hiss of air from the air vents broke the elegant silence of its interior. "All right!" Bucky grinned. "This is great!"

"Didn't you ever fly before?" One of the mission group, a pretty Asian girl, slid into the seat next to him.

"Boy, not a big widebody like this." Bucky had turned to gaze at the expanse of plane behind him, but the girl captured his attention. He fumbled for words. "How about you?"

Even her laugh seemed to have a little bit of Asian accent. "Several times. I was born in Thailand, and we lived there for many years. So I am, I guess you say, going home again."

Bucky's eyes widened with interest. "Wow! That's really something. What's your name?"

"Vasana." With slim fingers she fastened her belt. "I guess we're next to each other the whole way."

FIVE

JOURNEY INTO NIGHT

The steady hum of the DC-10's engines powered the Adventist group over the scenic mountains surrounding Anchorage. "Man, that is some view!" Bucky whistled as he finished off the last bites of his vegetarian meal. "Can you see all right?"

"Yes." The Thai girl cocked her head, peering past him at the sunset as it spilled over the snowy mountain ranges.

"I should let you sit here."

"No, your legs are too long to sit in the middle," she protested.

The sun had just settled behind the craggy mountains when the huge plane took off again, bound for Seoul. Bucky listened, fascinated, as the flight crew repeated the pre-flight announcements in several

Asian languages. "Which one's Thai?"

"Right now," Vasana smiled. "You keep hearing that word, '*kah*'? That is a Thai politeness ending most of our sentences." A buzz of foreign conversation filled the airplane as the craft taxied down the runway.

"Tell me your name again."

"Vasana." She pronounced the first consonant with a "w" sound.

"How do you spell that?"

An expectant little smile. "V-A-S-A-N-A."

He wrinkled his nose. "How come you say it like it's a 'w' instead of a 'v'?"

She gave a little laugh. "That is the Thai way. 'V' sounds like 'w' and 'w' sounds like 'v.' "

Bucky filed the interesting fact away for later. "I guess it'll be dark the rest of the way now," he mused, "since we're going east to west. That's what my dad said."

"Yeah, but wait till you see this." Gordon poked his head over the back of the seats.

"What do you mean?"

"Just watch."

The airline climbed higher and higher in the Alaskan sky. "Now right there on the horizon."

Bucky stared through the window where the sun had disappeared moments before. "Here it comes," the man murmured in a low voice.

Slowly, almost eerily, the setting sun began to climb up above the horizon, just barely clearing the distant line of snowy peaks.

"Awesome!" Bucky couldn't believe his eyes. "The sun went down, and now it's coming up again!"

"We're so far north that when the plane gets high

enough you can see past where the sun just went down. I saw it once before." The youth director spoke almost reverently.

"That's unreal." Bucky looked over at Vasana, who was transfixed by the sight. Slowly the sun sank—for the second time—as the Delta jet climbed to 35,000 feet.

The next nine hours were a marathon stretch of flying. An old movie danced across the screen but Bucky couldn't keep his eyes open. "Try to get some sleep." Gordon made his way down the aisle of the plane, giving encouragement to each young person.

After what seemed an eternity in a plane that was starting to feel smaller and more claustrophobic by the minute, the captain announced the descent into Seoul. Stirring from his drowsy nap, Bucky felt a sense of excitement course through him. "I'm really looking forward to seeing what everything looks like over here."

"At night from the sky it looks just like any other city," Vasana pointed out, peering over his shoulder at the approaching lights.

The row of Adventist students slowly filed out of the plane. Some of them were rubbing their eyes. "Man, I could not sleep!" Benny complained to one of the girls.

"Hey, back home it's already Monday morning," she retorted.

"And here's it's Monday night now."

"Huh?" Bucky had a confused look.

"We just crossed the dateline," Benny explained. "We just hopped from Sunday night to Monday night, you guys."

The airline terminal was nearly deserted. Bucky

wandered down the hallway, staring at the odd-looking Korean signs.

"What do you think?"

He looked up to see Pastor Humboldt approaching him.

"Boy, just like that, and you're in the Orient."

The youth director grinned. "Yeah. It's kind of weird, isn't it?"

Moments later the loudspeaker burst forth with a Korean announcement. "Get used to the feeling, Bucky," Gordon laughed. "We're a long way from home."

The next four hours of flying dragged by with more napping and an unwanted meal. "My body's so messed up I can't eat," he complained to Vasana, who was picking delicately at her plate.

"Just three more hours," Gordon announced to the students as the plane took off from Taiwan after another brief stop. "Is this the longest night you've ever been in?"

"Really!" One of the girls glanced at her watch. "I keep moving this back, but we're just hanging in space here. It's always midnight."

The final miles slipped away underneath the DC-10. The huge aircraft was almost silent in the darkness. Most of the passengers dozed quietly.

At last Bucky felt the aircraft dip slightly. "Almost there," he murmured to the Thai girl. "I keep forgetting that even though this seems like another universe to me, you're almost home now."

"Yes." Vasana had a quietly precise way of speaking. Her dark eyes seemed to glimmer with emotion as she spotted the occasional lights on the ground far below.

"What are those?"

"Village lights, I think. Maybe boats."

Bucky glanced down at his watch and pulled out the adjustment knob. "The way I figured it, it's just about one in the morning now," he groaned. "Is it . . . what? *Tuesday* morning? What?"

"Yep. Tuesday." Gordon stood up and glanced around. "Ten in the morning back home. Still yesterday morning there."

"Weird," Bucky commented for the umpteenth time.

A quiet burst of applause filled the cabin as the plane touched down on Bangkok soil. The students crowded around the windows as they pulled up to the gate.

"OK, kids, let's move out. Check for everything you brought on board."

The weary group of student missionaries walked unsteadily toward the exit and into the empty terminal. "Man, no one here," Benny grunted as he lugged a huge knapsack with one arm.

"Well, let's get our bags, everyone, and move through customs as quick as we can."

It took a good 45 minutes before the students finished with their legal paperwork. A short Thai official stamped passport after passport, beaming at each student. "Welcome to Thailand," he repeated in broken English.

"*Kop kuhn, kah*," Vasana murmured as she finished.

He lit up. A long stream of Thai burst forth. Vasana smiled and responded in the language. Bucky listened in fascination.

"Come on, guys, our bus is here." The 18 students

straggled outside into the humid air.

"Can you believe it's 1:00 in the morning?" Bucky mopped at his forehead. "It's hot here!"

Despite his fatigue, he gazed out the window at the busy traffic as they headed toward the Adventist hospital in downtown Bangkok. The diminutive bus driver, perched on the right-hand side of the vehicle, expertly darted in and out of the still congested traffic. Raucous *tuk tuks,* little three-wheeled taxis, beeped their horns and cut in front of the bus at every corner. *Boy,* he thought, *will I have lots to write Lisa about.*

"Everything's backward here, isn't it?" Gordon grinned, trying to buoy up the group. "Driver's on the right and the bus goes on the left."

Finally the vehicle pulled into a darkened mission compound. BANGKOK ADVENTIST HOSPITAL flickered in neon above the entrance.

"Well, it's a hospital. They must have beds," Bucky joked, nearly exhausted.

A tall man wearing a short-sleeved shirt and slippers walked up to the van and poked his head inside. "Are these our newest missionaries?" There was a murmur of response.

"Well, we've got places for everybody," the administrator smiled. "The girls will be staying in the west wing of the hospital, and you fellows, we've got plenty of floor space with one of our missionaries."

It seemed like just minutes later that sunlight streamed through an open window and nudged Bucky into consciousness. "Where . . . where am I?"

Benny gave him a nudge. "Get up, my man." He stretched. "You are away out here in *muang thai.*" Then he grinned broadly at Bucky's groggy expression.

Trying to rub the sleep out of his eyes, Bucky asked, "Where'd you learn that?"

The tall Black student motioned with his head. "Dr. Geltje's servant taught me."

A friendly woman poked her head into the living room. "Good morning, boys," she beamed in a strong European accent. "Anyone for some breakfast?"

"I could do with a shower," Bucky muttered.

"Well, we can find you a bath after we eat," the doctor smiled. "Radree has your breakfast ready."

Bucky waited until the physician had left and then slipped into his jeans. "What's there to eat?"

A huge bowl of sweetened "sticky rice" and pineapple slices soon altered the students' mood. "I guess I won't starve after all," Brandon, one of the boys traveling from Los Angeles, laughed. "But two weeks with no Dodger scores—man, I don't know."

"Hey, Dodgers got whupped yesterday," Benny asserted.

"How do you know that?"

"The doctor gets the paper here. Printed in English and everything. Giants beat the Dodgers 8 to 2."

"Wow." Bucky had to laugh. "Here you think you're way out in the mission field, and they've got all the ball scores."

"Well, come on, you guys, get ready. We got a train to catch tonight, and I want to do some sight-seeing." Benny scooted his chair back. "Radree, honey, that was good food! *Aroy mahk!*"

"How'd you learn that so fast?" Bucky groaned again, impressed.

Another huge grin. "I have a flair for languages," the tall student replied with a cosmopolitan smirk.

"Oh, boy!" Bucky headed for the shower.

Even in a pair of shorts and a tank top, Bucky had a blistering day of souvenir-hunting as the students trekked from one tourist site to another. Having exchanged just a little bit of money at the hospital cashier's office, he carefully bought a little trinket for Rachel Marie.

"Now stay together!" Gordon emphasized as they walked through a crowded alley. "You get lost here, and I don't know how we'd ever find you again."

"How's this money work again?" one of the girls wanted to know as they paused at a long row of tiny shops.

"Just figure about 25 baht to one dollar," Bucky told her. "A baht's about four cents at the moment."

"So we can ride the bus for just 12 cents?"

"Yeah. Not bad, huh?"

The noon sun beat down on the students as they gawked at a huge golden Buddha lying on its side. "That's called the Reclining Buddha," Gordon told the group. "You always read about idols in the Second Commandment? Well, here's one of the biggies of all time."

"Hey, look! McDonald's!" Terrie, one of the Portland girls, chirped in delight. "They've got McDonald's here."

"Come on," Bucky laughed. "We didn't fly clear over here to go to McDonald's."

The group did stop in for hot fudge sundaes after sampling some local concoctions at a nearby Thai restaurant. "Ah, a little taste of home," Benny grinned. " 'Cept they have hot mango pies instead of apple!"

Bucky looked over at Vasana. "What do you like better? Thai food or this ice cream."

She gave him a quiet smile. "Both."

The blazing heat did subside a bit as the afternoon wore on. Bucky found a store with exquisite postcards for sale. He dickered in good humor with the clerk and managed to get two for what the man had originally announced as the price for one.

"Way to hang tough, Stone!" Benny laughed.

"Just saved myself four baht!"

"Hey, these guys *want* you to bargain with 'em," the other teenage boy laughed. "They're disappointed if you just cave in. You just tell them, '*pang mahk*.' That means 'too expensive!' "

Bucky scribbled messages to Rachel Marie and Lisa and dropped the cards in the mail at the hospital's main office, admiring the colorful Thai stamps as he did so. "You'll probably get home before those cards do," Gordon grinned. "But it's the thought that counts."

That evening the bus took the students and Pastor Humboldt over to the train station for the overnight ride to Chiang Mai. Luggage cart handlers and food vendors pestered travelers as they made their way down the long platform looking for their railroad cars.

"Here we are!" Gordon examined the pink ticket slips. "Everybody hop on."

Bucky helped Vasana hoist her suitcase into the sleeping car, then climbed aboard. Rows of blue seats facing each other ran down both sides of the long compartment.

"Do we sit up all night on these?" one of the girls asked. She was a short, stocky junior from Phoenix.

Gordon grinned. "No, Ricki, they make these up into beds later on."

"Good," she sighed. "After that plane ride, I can't

afford to kiss another night of sleep goodbye."

The train started with a lurch and slowly pulled out of the Bangkok suburbs. The student missionaries lined the windows and watched the crowded traffic slip by.

"Look, there's the hospital!" Bucky pointed. "Man, we could have just hopped on right here."

"We're goin' slow enough we almost could." Benny gawked at the crowded street scene. "Look at that bus there. Those guys are hanging right off the end."

As the long train crawled north, Gordon pulled a guitar out of its case. "Let's have worship," he announced. "What shall we sing?"

The next half hour was a marathon music fest as the 18 students belted out their favorites. Benny, in particular, seemed to know every youth song ever invented, including one or two the rest hadn't heard before.

"I can't believe you guys," he complained with a big grin. "Where ya been all your lives?"

"Well, some of these oddball verses you come up with, I admit I've never heard before either." Gordon set down his guitar with a laugh. "I guess we've tormented the other passengers enough."

Bucky looked around. Sure enough, a number of the Thais on board had pressed close to listen. One, catching Bucky's eye, gave a nod and broad smile of appreciation. "Very good," the man said, proud of his English.

"Anybody have anything they want to share before we have prayer?" Gordon scanned the group of kids. There was a long silence.

"Yeah." Everyone looked over at Carl, one of the

quieter members of the group.

"Go ahead."

Slowly the student shared an experience from summer camp, where one of the primary campers had told him about physical abuse at home.

One of the girls shook her head sympathetically as Carl related the painful story, concluding, "So I hope you guys will pray for Stevie. He's really in a messed-up situation."

"We sure will." Gordon nodded soberly. "Anybody else?"

Two or three others made prayer requests before everybody separated into small bands of three. The quiet ding-ding-ding of a railroad crossing bell punctuated the silence as Bucky and two girls prayed for the success of the mission trip and for the various requests.

After the prayers, Benny glanced at his watch. "I ain't goin' to bed until I whip *somebody* in this train in a game of Rook." He dug in his duffel bag for the little orange cards. "Who's going to take me on?"

Several students eagerly gathered around to play. Bucky crowded close, watching the spirited action. Benny, despite his easygoing nature, had a fantastic memory, seeming to know just what cards were left to be played. He and his partner won three games in a row.

"Ahhhh, that feels great," Benny sighed as one of the girls standing behind him began to massage his broad shoulders. "Baby, I am *in love!*"

She grinned. "I'll trade this for you showing me how you play so good."

Benny looked up at the others. "Come on, Stone, get in here. I need a fresh face to beat."

"I never played this before."

"Aaaah, it's easy. Just hold your cards where I can always peek at them, and I'll tell you what to play." Benny's big laugh boomed through the passenger car.

A gust of wind blew through the window, threatening to scatter the cards. Bucky managed to stumble through a round of play without making any major mistakes, but once again Benny's team came away with nearly all of the points. "Like taking candy from a baby!" the big student grinned.

Bucky felt a soft pair of hands on his shoulders. Looking up, he saw Vasana standing behind him. "Boy, you'll be my friend for life," he grinned as she kneaded his stiff muscles. "I was sore from that plane ride."

Her slim Oriental fingers continued to massage him through the next game. He shot her a grateful look as she finished. "That was great." Then he paused. "How about you now?"

A tiny look of formality crossed her face. "Oh . . . no, thank you." She silently moved away.

A frown crossed Bucky's face. He looked over to where the young girl sat alone by the window watching the darkened landscape whiz by. A memory of Lisa flickered in his mind. He needed to write her a letter.

"Bedtime, boys and girls," Gordon announced as the porter came down the aisle. Moving with swift efficiency, the man converted seats into upper and lower berths.

"Where's the restroom?" Ricki wanted to know.

"Down at the end." Gordon pointed. "It isn't much of one, though. And if you're going down to brush your teeth, remember, don't use their water."

"What do I do?"

He handed her a plastic bottle. "Just take a bit of this," he advised. "Some folks drink the water here and get away with it. But let's not take any chances."

Bucky eased himself into the cramped upper berth and slipped out of his jeans. By lying on his side at an angle he could almost . . . He sighed.

Even with the raucous cries of snack vendors at the train's several nocturnal stops along the way, Bucky awoke refreshed the next morning. "I guess my jet lag's about done," he grinned in relief as he greeted the youth director.

"Have some pineapple." Gordon motioned toward a heaping plate. "All this for a buck. Can you imagine? My treat."

"Thanks." Bucky savored the juicy fruit. "How soon do we get to Chiang Mai?"

"'Bout an hour."

SIX

"MAN, WE ARE IN THE JUNGLE!"

The Chiang Mai train station was less crowded than its Bangkok counterpart, but still full of Oriental bustle. Eager merchants dangled flower necklaces, hotel brochures, and offers of "Taxi? Taxi?" in front of the 18 students and Pastor Humboldt.

At the front entrance a young Thai man stepped forward. "Pastor Humboldt?"

"Yes." The youth director offered his hand. "You're Pastor Sawat?"

A big smile. "Hello. We are so glad to have you here." His English was nearly perfect.

"Well, here are our kids." Gordon motioned toward the blue-jeaned group. "And ready to work!"

"Welcome to Chiang Mai." The same broad grin. Pastor Sawat brought both hands together in the traditional Thai *"wai"* greeting. *"Sawatdee."* He motioned toward a young woman next to him. "This is my wife, Kobkeow."

Gordon went down the list, introducing each young person to their Thai host and hostess. The pastor repeated each name, as did his wife. "Buck-EE," she said, accenting the second syllable instead of the first, when Gordon came to Bucky.

"My wife is still learning English," Sawat beamed. He looked at Vasana. "We are so happy to see Vasana again after several years."

"Are we ready?" Gordon asked.

"Yes, let's go." The pastor directed them toward a dilapidated bus. "Not as fancy as you may have in California." He pronounced his words carefully. "Are you all from California?"

"Oh, no, from all over. These kids came from everywhere to help build your dormitory."

The pastor smiled his gratitude. "As you say, 'All aboard!' "

The drive to the academy took about an hour as the road led further and further away from civilization. Even as they turned off the main road, however, Bucky still spotted a road sign advertising Coca-Cola.

"Man, we are in the *jungle*." Benny poked his head out the window. "*Hot* in the jungle, too."

The academy campus was isolated several kilometers away from any other signs of life. Six buildings dotted the hilly terrain, and dirt paths divided the grounds into rough green sections.

"Welcome to Mae Dhang." Pastor Sawat surveyed the campus. "We only have a few students here now. Most of them return in three weeks. I know how eager they will be to have the new dormitory."

"Where do we put everybody?" Gordon asked.

The young Thai minister pointed. "The boys can use the dormitory over there. We've cleared out most of the students' belongings, and there are just two boys here now. They're staying on the other side. The girls can sleep in the chapel."

"Are the teachers here?"

Pastor Sawat shook his head. "Three of them are away for their vacation time, and our principal returned to Australia for the summer. He and his family come from there."

"Who's heading up this building project?" Gordon had a worried look that the short pastor noticed immediately.

"Oh, the foreman will be here this afternoon. His name is Prasert. He will lead in the building project."

"Good." The youth director sighed in relief. "I know a little bit about building, but not enough to run the show."

"This man, Prasert, is very skilled," Sawat asserted. "His English is not so good, maybe, but he can show you what to do."

"Terrific." Gordon glanced at the sky, then turned to his group of young people. "Let's get settled and see about some lunch. After that we'll get some work in. Start earning our keep!"

* * *

The foreman was large, at least for a Thai. Bucky, at six-feet-four, was just a few inches taller than the supervisor. Prasert had a cheerful smile that revealed several gold teeth.

"So glad to seeing you," he repeated over and over until the girls snickered. Taking everybody out to the building site, he issued several simple instructions.

"This part done," he said simply, pointing to the concrete foundation. "Now frame and paint. Some brick here." He pointed to a set of plans that were remarkably precise. Bucky, looking over his shoulder, recognized some of the same specifications often used at the home repair center back in Hampton Beach.

"You boys. Here." He drew some simple designs, illustrating how they should do the framing. "Three days, making frame. OK?" The students nodded their assent.

Even in one afternoon the mission crew made good progress. Prasert moved among the young people, pointing out new assignments or ways to improve what they were doing. Every suggestion ended with the same "OK?" Several of the girls helped mix mortar and sort supplies, anticipating what the framers would need.

"Very good! Very good!" The gold-toothed smile flashed as the foreman struggled to pronounce his r's.

"*Dee mahk!*" Benny looked up from his hammering.

"Yes! *Dee mahk!*" Prasert seemed delighted with the American boy's attempt to speak the language. "*Dee mahk* is very good!"

"All right!" Bucky reached over and gave his friend a high five. "By Sabbath you'll be translating the sermon."

That night the students feasted on a huge pile of mangoes and a tiny fruit Bucky had never seen before but that tasted similar to grapes. "Try this stuff!"

Gordon advised. "*Linchee*, they call it. Better than back home."

The youth director's guitar provided lively accompaniment once again as the mission group sang their favorites from back home. Bucky grinned as he saw the academy's few remaining students slip in and join the Americans.

"Welcome!" Gordon waved a greeting at them. "Come sing with us!"

One of the girls shook her head shyly.

"Do you speak English?" She shook her head again.

The youth director turned toward Vasana. "Ask them if they know any songs."

The girl spoke to the Thai students in a rapid stream or words. Smiles came to their faces as they answered. "They know 'Lift Up the Trumpet,'" she told Gordon.

"Let's sing that." He strummed a few chords. "Tell them to sing along in Thai."

The mixture of languages drifted out across the jungle surrounding the campus. With Vasana's help, the students managed to find several songs they knew in common. Bucky noticed with a grin that the Thai students' favorites were all "oldies" from years ago.

After prayer, the group split up. "No wandering off!" Gordon ordered. "You kids stay close to home."

Even though it was nearly dark, a Rook game started up under a 60-watt bulb hanging from an outdoor lamppost. Bucky watched for a few minutes, then turned as he saw Vasana approaching him.

"There is a lake right over this hill," she told him in her precise way. "Do you want to see it?" Her Oriental face was solemn.

He grinned. "Sure." After scanning the horizon, he said, "Getting kind of dark. Will we be able to see anything?"

"Yes, I think so."

He followed the slim girl as they walked up the path. In his mind Bucky contrasted Vasana's upscale Western attire with the simple costumes worn by the Thai girls and realized what a difference culture made.

In the twilight they watched the gentle ripples of the darkened lake. Mosquitos buzzed around Bucky's head as the warm air gradually cooled off.

"What's it like being here again?" he asked her.

Vasana shrugged delicately. "Good, I guess."

"Did you ever live up here?"

"I was born here," she said quietly.

"Did you go to school in Chiang Mai?"

She shook her head. "In Bangkok."

"How'd you know the pastor then?"

She plucked a blade of grass and pulled it apart. "He went to college there. My father met him there many years ago when I was very small."

"Your dad's a doctor, right?"

The girl nodded.

"How'd you come to be in America?"

Vasana looked away before answering. "He studied for his medical examinations, but then could not take them on Sabbath. So he waited for the next year, and they were on Sabbath again. Many people tried to change the day of the testing, but they could not. Finally some friends helped him to come to America and complete his final training there."

Bucky digested the information. "Now that he's finished, what does he want to do?"

The young girl shivered in the cool tropical air. "He doesn't know," she said simply. "Maybe come back here someday. Maybe not." She paused. "Maybe it is hard to live in America and then come live here again."

An image of affluent California with its Disneyland and malls popped into Bucky's mind. Right at that moment it seemed a million miles away from the primitive Thai landscape surrounding them.

Thursday and Friday were long work days for the 18 young people. With Prasert's help the framing went well. Bucky and Benny remarked often how the Thai builder had an uncanny ability to spot mistakes before they happened.

"You, how you say, connecting joint *this* way," he gently chided as one of the boys tried in vain to couple two sections of pipe. "Watch." A few simple directions set matters right. "OK?"

As quitting time approached Friday afternoon, Gordon drove up in the school's little jeep, shifting the gears awkwardly with his left hand. "Anybody do any work today?"

"Yeah," Bucky sighed, shaking his head and watching the beads of sweat fly off. "Tons of it."

"Thirsty?"

"You bet. All we can drink is that boiled water, and this morning the fridge went haywire. Prasert got it going again, but now the water's just lukewarm."

A mischievous gleam appeared in the youth director's eyes. "How's a cold Sprite sound?"

"I'd think I'd died and went to heaven," Benny declared, mopping his brow. "I know that ain't exactly kosher Adventism, but, man, it's hot."

Gordon reached behind him in the jeep and

flipped a familiar green can to the tall student. "Catch!"

"You got it!"

"One for everybody!" A big tub of ice held enough cold cans for each student. "Got 'em in town."

"All right!" Benny reached into the tub and pulled out a huge hunk of ice. "This is what I need." He rubbed the melting cube across his glistening dark skin. "Oh, baby."

Jo-Jo, one of the girls, grabbed a second cube, and, without warning, dropped it down the back of Benny's neck.

"Aaaargh!" He twisted around in pretended agony. "I know I'm hot, but gimme some warning!"

Moments later a free-for-all broke out as the students pelted each other with slivers of ice. Vasana was giggling as frantically as the rest as Bucky dropped a handful of cubes down the back of her T shirt.

* * *

That night the group gathered in the chapel. Bucky looked at the girls, now attired in simple dresses and freshly done hairdos. The dust and grime of the busy week were just a memory.

"Some of you may be wondering about that old black-and-white photo on the wall," the youth director said quietly as he began his devotional. "This little building is called Venden Chapel. That picture is of Dan Venden, one of the Adventist Church's great old evangelistic preachers. I was a pastoral intern under him when I first started in the ministry, way back before he passed away in 1973. He had a real love for this particular mission field. Two of his own daughters worked in the Orient for many years, and one of them right here in northern Thailand. After he retired, he contributed the money to build this chapel because he wanted to help young people just like you kids get an education here."

A murmur of interest spread among the young people. "We're going to celebrate Communion together," Gordon went on, picking up his Bible. "I know we're a long way from home, but as we share together these emblems, we can know that we're united in Jesus with other believers all around the world." He paused. "Including all the folks back home who helped send you out here to do the Lord's work."

Quietly they paired off to wash each other's feet and then take the tiny wafers and cups of grape juice the youth director had prepared. The Thai students stepped forward as well, following Vasana's whispered instructions.

Following prayer bands, the leader drew the group back together once again. "Tomorrow we're going to ride the bus back into Chiang Mai to attend church," he said. "And there's going to be a special surprise I think you're never going to forget."

Bucky sat in the chapel with the others for a little while, listening as Benny demonstrated some new chords on the guitar. A full moon rose over the mountain hillsides, spilling light onto the quiet campus.

For a moment he cocked his head to one side. What was that down by the path?

Slipping away from the group, he followed the moonlit trail toward the lower part of the academy campus. There, just off the pathway, was a simple tombstone. He bent down to make out the plain lettering: HELEN MORTON.

Mystified, he looked around, but no one was nearby. Suddenly he caught a glimpse of a slight figure heading across the hill toward the makeshift volleyball courts.

"Vasana! Wait for me!" He jogged over to the girl.

Despite her reserved demeanor, Bucky thought he sensed a flicker of interest. "Hello," she responded. "Where are you going?"

"Just to walk."

He paused. "Can I come along?"

"Of course." She motioned with her head. "Come."

As he followed her up the pathway, he tried to think of something to say. "How'd you like Communion?"

"It was good." She pointed to a small bench surrounded by trees and some wild flowers. "Would you like to sit here?"

"Sure." Sinking down on the hard wood, he looked at her. "Teach me some Thai." A short laugh. "I gotta keep up with Benny."

"What do you want to know how to say?"

"I don't know. How about just 'hello'?"

"Very easy. *Sawatdee.*"

"Oh, yeah." He nodded, then repeated it after her. "I've heard people say that a lot."

"Remember, a man must say" *'Sawatdee krahp.'* " She emphasized the final syllable.

"How come?"

"That is the proper way. A woman says, *'Sawatdee kah.'* "

"Oh, I get it."

He thought of several more words, and she dutifully translated them, a tiny smile curving her lips as she listened to his stiff American accent.

"Not too good, am I?"

"No, you do very well," she encouraged.

"How do you say 'Jesus'?"

She smiled. *"Prah Yesu."*

"Sort of sounds like Jesus," he commented.

"Yes. My father told me that the name of Jesus is very similar in all languages."

"Wow. I didn't know that."

The pair chatted easily for a number of minutes, pausing to swipe away a few mosquitos that hovered nearby.

"I wonder what's the big surprise tomorrow." Bucky watched a cloud slide across the moon. "Hey, I can see Orion. See? Right there? Man, just like back home."

The girl ignored his last remark. "Tomorrow will be very special," she said quietly.

"How come?"

She didn't answer.

SEVEN

DANGER IN THE RAIN

Pastor Sawat eased the dust-covered bus onto the academy campus and admired the partially constructed dormitory. "You have worked hard," he said.

"Uh huh," Ricki said as she climbed aboard. "I bet we'll finish ahead of schedule."

"Good!" The Thai pastor flashed his characteristic smile. "We are glad you are all coming to our church today."

The 18 students and their youth leader sang praise choruses as the bus rolled down the two-lane paved road toward Chiang Mai. Even at 8:15 in the morning trucks, motorcyclists, and a long stream of small foreign-made cars crowded the highway.

In town the bus pulled into a street bordering a long canal and entered a driveway near a small white building. "This is our church," Sawat announced. "Welcome to Sabbath School."

As the students entered the small building, Bucky watched with interest as the Thai members took off their shoes and left them at the door. "How come they're doing that?"

"Just the custom here." Gordon bent over and unloosed his own shoelaces. "How often do you get to go barefoot in church? Enjoy!"

Bucky padded in his stocking feet over to an empty chair next to Jo-Jo. In the row ahead of him, Vasana leaned over and said hello in Thai to an older woman, holding her hands together in the traditional greeting.

Pastor Sawat went to the front and made some announcements in Thai, then switched abruptly into English. "We wish a special welcome to our friends from America. They are building a dormitory for us at Mae Dhang and doing a fine job. We are so happy you are here." He nodded toward the group as Thai Sabbath School members turned to greet the students.

The pastor followed with one more announcement in Thai and then gave the name of the hymn they would sing. "What a Friend We Have in Jesus," he added for the benefit of the visitors.

Even though the hymnbooks were printed only in Thai, the students sang along with the choruses, relying on memory. After a short prayer, a young man with glasses stepped forward to teach the lesson. Pastor Sawat stood next to him, translating the lesson and questions into English.

" . . . And so in Christ we are all one people." The minister listened with a smile as the intense young teacher added one more comment. " . . . as we see here today with our brothers and sisters from so far away." A cheerful rumble of agreement swelled through the congregation.

The church service had barely begun when Pastor Sawat made a surprise announcement. "As most of you know—except for our visitors—we are not having our service here in this building today." Bucky frowned. Was this the surprise Gordon had mentioned?

"We are going up to the mountain as I promised," the pastor added. "Those of you with cars or *tuk tuks*, let us go. The bus will bring the students and any others who need a ride."

It took 15 minutes for the congregation to ride up the hill behind Chiang Mai and pull into a small grove near a rapidly flowing river. Along the banks the Adventist family gathered quietly, watching the white water rush past.

The short Thai pastor stepped forward, still wearing his dress trousers and white shirt, but without his shoes. Bucky looked puzzled as the man strode into the water near the edge of the bank, the current tugging at him.

When the water reached almost to his waist, he turned and faced the crowd. With his head bowed, he prayed briefly in Thai and then looked up.

"Today a very special moment has come," he began. "An old friend has returned to the land she loves, and today is the day of her baptism."

Bucky sucked in his breath as he glanced around. Making her way through the crowd, clad in a simple white dress, Vasana stepped gingerly into the water.

"Many years ago, Vasana's father became a Christian;" Sawat said, raising his voice so that all could hear. "Born among the opium families in the north, he escaped to Chiang Mai looking for work. Instead he found Jesus." He translated his own remarks into the national tongue.

"Now his daughter has returned to the very pool of water where her father was baptized. In this very spot when Vasana was a little girl of three years, her father and mother joined the Adventist family. Now Vasana, clear from America, has come home to Chiang Mai to do the same."

Bucky felt tears in his eyes as he watched the girl's face. The secret she had held locked in her heart throughout the whole trip now unfolded before her new friends.

The simple ceremony over, the group moved to a clearing and listened intently as Pastor Sawat, his clothes still dripping, shared a short message of hope. Switching easily between Thai and English, he concluded with a prayer for unity among God's world-wide family.

Bucky slipped over to where Vasana stood under a banana tree, her cotton dress almost dry in the warm Chiang Mai air. "Why didn't you tell us?" he whispered.

She smiled. "It was a secret."

"Pretty good." He leaned over and gave her an awkward one-arm hug. "I'm happy for you."

"Thanks." Her eyes still brimmed with emotion as the other students on the volunteer missions team offered hugs and congratulations.

"All aboard," Gordon announced. "We're going on a picnic!"

The students chattered happily as the bus crept higher up the mountain highway, stopping at a wide spot in the road.

"What's here?" Benny wanted to know.

"Listen!"

"What?"

The youth director pointed. "Right over there. See that waterfall?"

The students clambered out. "All right! Are we having lunch here?"

"Yep." Gordon and Bucky carried two huge bags of sandwiches and fruit over to a large spot of grass near the river's edge. The group devoured the food and then spread out to hike or wade in the cool water near the waterfall's edge.

"Check it out!" Carl stood directly under the pounding spray, letting the water drench him. "This feels great!"

"But now you're sopping wet," Bucky pointed out.

"Aaaah, who cares? Look how fast Vasana dried out."

With a grin, Bucky joined his friend under the falls, letting the pounding rush of water massage his head and shoulders. "Man, that does feel good." He beckoned to Vasana. "Get in here!"

"No!" She shook her head vigorously. "I just got dry."

"So get wet again."

Once more she shook her head.

"Do I have to come get you?"

She squealed. "Bucky!"

Moments later the three of them clung to each other under the spray. "See there," he grinned. "Ain't this great?"

She laughed, the drops of water dancing on her smooth brown skin.

That evening Bucky sat in on the regular Rook game, Vasana's hand resting on his shoulder as she watched the action. She pinched him when he inadvertently tossed the wrong card on the pile, sending his partner to a second defeat in a row.

"Come on, Stone!" Benny complained with a glare at his friend. "You are sinking our aircraft carrier, my man."

"Sorry." Bucky eyed the rest of his cards. "With Vasana here, I can't think straight." He looked up at her with a teasing smile.

Sunday morning the work routine started up once again. Under Prasert's watchful eye and Gordon's cheerful enthusiasm, the new dormitory was rapidly taking shape. Bucky and the rest of the crew, following the youth director's motto "Work hard, play hard!" dug in for long hours of labor under the hot Thai sun.

Wednesday morning the Thai building supervisor examined the structure with a critical eye. "Pretty good, huh?" Bucky felt a surge of pride.

"Yes, good." Prasert's gold teeth flashed. "But not done."

"We still have today and tomorrow."

"Yes." Prasert looked at the distant horizon and the clouds forming. "If no rain, we can finish."

An hour later the students learned the meaning of the word "monsoon." Without warning the heavens opened up, drenching everything in sight.

"Go quick! Cover!" Prasert shouted to the scurrying teenagers as they pulled tarps and plastic sheets over everything they could.

"Buck-EE!" Even after a week Prasert still emphasized the second syllable. "Run to truck and bring here. More covers!"

"Me?" Bucky mopped rain water out of his eyes.

"Yes! Go quick." The supervisor tossed the keys to Bucky.

Dashing through the downpour, he splashed toward the truck parked near the entrance to the campus. In the blinding torrent, it was difficult to see the path. He was three-quarters of the way when a tree root poking out of the soil tripped him up. With an agonized thud he hit the ground. Wet sod and leaves clung to his face as he twisted around and tried to clear his vision. A searing pain shot through his ankle.

With a gasp he sucked in his breath. Was it broken? He wiped the water and grime from his eyes and looked down at his left leg, the bare skin streaked with mud. Pulling himself to a sitting position he put a little weight on it. Again the sharp pain returned.

Fumbling around in the soft mud, he tried to find the keys he had dropped. All at once his heart began to pound. Perched in the driving rain less than five feet away from his injured leg was a long, ominous shape. Symmetrical rings of black and yellow scales slid slowly in a coil toward him.

His breath coming in little gasps, he tried again to climb to his feet, but the throbbing pain held him riveted in place.

"Snake!" In the roar of the monsoon rain, his voice sounded like a weakened squeak. "Snake!"

A good hundred feet away he could see a shadowy figure begin to move toward him. The tropical snake remained motionless as Bucky tried desperately to inch away.

"Help!" He gasped in fear. A memory from an encyclopedia back home sent fresh tremors of panic through him. *Yellow and black stripes—deadly poisonous.*

"Buck-EE!" It was the voice of the foreman. "Do not be moving."

"I won't." His voice shook. For the moment at least, the driving rain was holding the viper at bay. "What should I do?"

"Stay very still." Prasert's cotton T-shirt stuck to his broad chest in the downpour. "Say nothing." Moving with instincts honed by years in the tropical jungle, the man picked up a large stick and slipped in behind the snake.

"Bucky." Standing about ten yards away, Vasana's quiet voice reached his ears. "Bucky, don't move."

He nodded imperceptibly. Somehow the girl's words had a calming effect. He could feel his pounding heartbeat slow just a little bit. Taking a deep breath, he glanced over at the sinister stripes.

"Quiet now." Prasert's whispered words were barely audible in the hiss of the rain as he edged closer and closer, the huge stick poised in his hand.

Ten feet . . . nine . . . eight. Without warning the snake began to move forward, slithering rapidly toward Bucky's exposed leg.

With a shout Prasert darted forward, bringing the club down on the snake's body close to the head. Twisting away, the viper's body trembled for a moment, then continued toward the crippled teenage boy.

"Bhai!" The harsh word froze Bucky's heart. Mesmerized with fear, he watched as the construction

foreman rushed forward again. Twisting the club under the snake's body, he flipped the deadly serpent away from Bucky. The yellow-and-black coils sailed through the air, landing in the path a good 30 feet away.

"Bucky!" With a sob, the Thai girl rushed to his side. "Are you all right?"

His body shaking, he sank to the ground in relief. "Yeah." He clutched at her.

"Look!" She pointed to the path where Prasert landed a well-aimed blow at the snake's head. The stunned viper shook momentarily, then lay still. A second and third blow finished the job.

"*Dhai lao!*" With a note of satisfied triumph, the powerfully built foreman raised the stick aloft.

"What's that mean?" Bucky's voice was still weak.

"*Dhai*. What does that sound like?"

He forced a tired grin. "*Dhai*. I dunno. Die? Dead?"

"Uh huh."

The pounding rain was already easing as Prasert approached the couple. "Buck-EE. You are all right?"

"Yeah." With Vasana's help he struggled to get to his feet. "I just hurt my ankle a little bit." When he tested it, he found the pain definitely easing.

"Very close with snake." The man spoke matter-of-factly. "Banded krite. Poison."

"I know." Bucky held out a hand. "Thanks."

Prasert smiled. "Never mind truck now. Rain gone."

When Bucky looked up at the sky, he could see blue patches already starting to appear as the rain clouds passed to the north.

"You can walking?"

"Uh huh. I think so." Vasana slipped an arm around him as he began hobbling back to the group. "Wait! The keys!"

It took just a moment to find them gleaming in the mud. The student group applauded as he approached them. "That man'll do anything to get a pretty girl to hold him up," Benny declared, giving his friend a high five.

The building foreman clapped softly. "Rain gone. Now we work harder?"

It soon became apparent that the rain had made the entire dormitory project a race against time. The tired workers toiled by lamplight until 9:30 that evening and started again at dawn the next day.

"Train pulls out at 6:30 tonight," Gordon grimaced as he helped plaster the east wall. "Come on, guys!"

Even with his slightly sore ankle, Bucky worked furiously with Benny to complete the roof as Prasert scurried from one side to the other, barking cheerful orders. "Everyone doing good! We make it OK. I think!" He laughed as he checked a door's hinges, then nodded approval to the perspiring boys.

At 4:00 Bucky laid down his tools with a sigh of relief. "Done!"

"Very good! Very good!" Prasert repeated over and over. "Everything done OK."

"*Dee mahk!*" Benny tried to give the Thai supervisor a high five.

"Yes. *Dee mahk!*" The students congratulated each other.

Gordon and Pastor Sawat, both dripping with perspiration as well, shook hands with the grinning builder, then motioned for the volunteer group to gather around.

"I'm so proud of you kids," Gordon said quietly. "Just a tremendous job all the way. Especially last night and today."

"Yes," nodded the Thai pastor. "Thank you, young people. This dormitory will serve our Thai young people for many years to come." He laughed. "If the roof ever leaks, we will have you come back to Chiang Mai and fix it!"

"No way!" Benny shook his head. "Me and Buck did that roof right!" Everybody laughed.

Gordon motioned for silence. "Pastor Sawat has made a suggestion I think is excellent. What if we let this dormitory be called Helen Morton Hall?"

The name triggered a memory in Bucky's mind and he strained to remember where he had heard it before.

Ricki beat him to the question. "Who's that?"

Pastor Sawat's eyes sobered. "Dr. Morton came to Thailand to work for our people," he said quietly. "From America. She worked here alone. Her family was all in America. For many years she lived here in the small house by the path."

Suddenly Bucky remembered the tombstone. "What happened to her?" he asked.

"Robbers." The pastor's voice was heavy with grief, as if remembering it again. "Robbers came here and killed her. They shot her on the steps of her house."

One of the girls winced, clapping her hand to her mouth. "Oh, no! How sad!"

"Yes. Very sad." Sawat nodded. "She was a good friend to Thai people. Now her grave is here, very far from her home and family." He paused. "But she has home and family here with us."

During the long silence Bucky thought again of the lonely grave so far from the United States.

"What do you think, kids?" Gordon broke the tension. "The Helen Morton Hall?"

"For sure." Bucky spoke for the group. "Moved, seconded, all in favor say 'aye.' " With one voice, it carried unanimously.

"We will put up a sign on the wall. Helen Morton Hall, built by volunteer young people from America." The pastor's eyes shone with gratitude.

It was a tired but satisfied group that said goodbye to Pastor Sawat and Prasert at the train station that evening. "Come back to Thailand again!" The two Thais waved until the long blue train had almost pulled out of view.

EIGHT

"R AND R" IN BANGKOK

The monotonous clicking of the metal wheels on the track beneath the railroad car lulled Bucky into a state of thoughtful solitude. He looked around the crowded passenger area at his new friends. There was Benny, strumming a "hot lick" on Pastor Humboldt's guitar, laughing boisterously as he butchered the lyrics to a popular song. Ricki with her short, staccato laugh and variety of "funny noises" she could mimic. Carl's quiet grin. Jo-Jo's endless storehouse of pranks, mostly played on Benny.

The moonlight danced its way through the thick glass window and cast shadows on the wall as he reflected on their week of work and fellowship. Day after day of mingling and sweating together with fellow believers. Eighteen kids—all of them Adventists just like him . . .

And yet there was Dan. And Sam. Solid guys who had found the Lord because he had gone to public school. And somewhere up in Washington, a pretty girl named Lisa who, because of Bucky's influence, at least was thinking about what part Jesus should have in her life.

His eyes fell on Vasana. Perched on the arm of her seat, she gazed idly at the "Go Fish" game that was just starting, but her thoughts seemed far away.

For a moment Bucky almost went over to talk with her. But something held him back. Memories of high school . . . Lisa . . . Deirdre. Girls and romance led to such turmoil, especially when religion was a factor. And now here was Vasana, so different from anyone he had ever known.

"Have a soda." Gordon dangled an orange-flavored soft drink in front of him. "It's on me."

"Oh . . . uh, thanks." With a grin he accepted it.

The youth director leaned against the seat next to Bucky's. "How's your ankle?"

"Oh, it's fine. Feels good as new."

"That's good." Gordon took a sip of his own drink. "You guys did a great job. Boy, I never thought we'd finish on time."

"It was fun." Bucky looked over to where Benny was just practicing another Thai expression on a startled passerby. "Pretty hard work, though. You're right."

"Well, I just wanted you to know how much I appreciated it, Bucky." The director put a friendly arm around the young man's shoulder. "I think you cranked out as much work as anyone on the team, and I'm real grateful."

Bucky shot the minister an appreciative look.

The night in the too-short sleeping compartment dragged by this time. No sleeping position was comfortable for very long, and two compartments down, Benny and Ricki seemed to be engaged in a never-ending argument about some extremely insignificant point.

"Can it, you guys!" Bucky's whisper seemed to quiet them at least for the moment.

* * *

"Where to?" Benny surveyed the pile of luggage on the Bangkok train platform. "Now that the heavy stuff is done, what do we do for the rest of the trip?"

"I got a surprise for you." Gordon waved to the hospital's bus driver who had just entered the terminal. "Grab your stuff and let's go."

Despite the group's persistent questioning, the youth director refused to offer any hints. The crowded bus snaked its way through the hot and hazy mid-morning Bangkok traffic.

"Man, this is worse than California freeways even," Bucky marveled, watching a city bus lurching by. The crowded blue vehicle was jammed with human cargo, mostly standing in the aisles and on the boarding steps. "Can you imagine going to work like that every day?"

The little hospital bus eased down a side road and pulled into a large complex shielded by a large wall. "Where are we, man?" Benny poked his head out the window.

"After hard work in the mission field, it's customary to enjoy some 'R and R,'" Gordon beamed.

"How does some swimming sound to you?"

"All right!" In the relentless August heat the huge Olympic-sized pool looked like paradise to the 18 fatigued young people.

"How'd you line this up?" Bucky dived into the cool water and surfaced next to Gordon.

"Well, this is kind of an exclusive club here, but we managed to work it out. When the management heard about your trip to Chiang Mai to help their people, they said, 'Come on over.'"

"This is great." Bucky waved to Carl who was perched on the 10-meter board high above the surface. "Go for it!"

The shy youth hesitated, then executed a perfect one-and-a-half tuck somersault, cutting the water's surface with barely a ripple.

"Wow! Did you see that?" He turned in time to spot Vasana coming out of the ladies' locker room, clad in a simple one-piece suit that accentuated her slim figure.

The relaxing Friday hours slipped away as the students basked in the luxuries of the club. In addition to the full-length pool, it had badminton courts, ping pong, and even a full golf course.

"I'd shoot a round of golf, 'cept I haven't got any clubs," Benny complained, eyeing the vast expanse of closely-cropped green grass.

"They'll rent you some," Gordon responded.

Benny shook his head. "Naaah. Too hot. I better stay here and be lifeguard in case some of our girls want to drown or something." He laughed.

The sun was nearing the horizon as the happy mission team climbed back on the bus and rode through town to the Adventist hospital. Dr. Geltje welcomed the boys into her living room once again and set out a feast of doughnuts and tropical fruit.

"How long have you worked here at this hospital," Bucky asked her as he polished off the last bite of the pastry.

The woman pondered. "Let's see. I came here from the hospital in Singapore back in . . . I guess I've been here just about 10 years now."

"Are you kidding?" Bucky shook his head. "Don't you miss home?"

"This is my home," she said quietly.

"But what about . . . what is it, Denmark?"

"That's home, too," the doctor conceded. "But when you grow to love the people here, you find yourself thinking of this country as home. When I go home to Denmark on furlough, I end up missing Thailand."

Carl cut himself another slice of mango. "It's an awful hot place to live."

Dr. Geltje's face crinkled into a smile. "That's what our visitors always say. There's an old missionary joke that says there are three seasons in Thailand: hot, hotter, and hottest."

"Really." Benny nodded in agreement. "And we all came during 'hottest.' "

"Yes, you did." The doctor glanced up at the ceiling where the spinning fan blew a gentle breeze down on them. "But we soon learn to adjust. My bedroom, at least, has air conditioning in it. So it's nice and cool in there. And we dress for this kind of weather." She laughed. "I can't remember the last time I wore a pair of nylons. We just never do around here."

The next morning Bucky and the boys met the

girls at the door of the hospital church. The fully-enclosed building was air conditioned and quiet, providing a Sabbath haven from the shimmering tropical temperatures and the incessant traffic grinding by on the street just outside the compound.

The Sabbath School superintendent beamed when he saw the two rows of American students. "Welcome to Bangkok! We are glad to have so many visitors."

Gordon stood and briefly explained the group's recent mission. "We return home to the U.S. Monday morning, but we're happy to enjoy a weekend here in Bangkok before leaving."

The superintendent whispered something to someone else on the platform before responding. "We are hoping . . . maybe you could do something special for our Sabbath School today. Sing a special song, perhaps?"

A reluctant murmur came from the pews, but Gordon nodded his head with a big smile. "I'm sure they'd be delighted!" Everyone laughed.

"No way!" Benny shook his head in protest.

"Oh, you guys. Come on." The youth director reached for his guitar. "We'll just sing one of our praise choruses for them."

Putting on a smile, Bucky went up to the platform with the others, nudging Benny as he turned to face the congregation. "Just shut up and sing," he whispered.

Benny scanned the largely female audience made up of student nurses. "Yeah, I just changed my mind," he replied.

The student group managed to sing a passable version of one of their vesper favorites and even came up with some good harmony on the chorus. Nods from the nurses rewarded the singers. Bucky saw one of the younger girls blush and whisper to her seatmate as she eyed the guys in the back row of the singing group.

After church Gordon called the students together. "They're going to give us lunch in the cafeteria," he announced. "Then I thought we'd maybe do just a little bit of singing for a few of the patients here in the hospital, and afterward you can have some free time. OK?"

"I didn't hear nothin' after you said the word 'lunch,' " Benny declared. "Let's do that first."

* * *

It was after the singing that Vasana approached Bucky. "There is a temple very near the hospital," she said. "Noelle and I want to see it. Maybe you could come?" Somehow the week in Thailand had brought back some of her Oriental reserve. The invitation seemed to spring from a reluctant shyness.

"Sure." Bucky pulled off his necktie. "You don't think Gordon'll mind?"

"Could you ask him?"

Bucky explained the brief excursion to the youth director.

"Oh, I think that's OK. But you kids watch yourselves. Don't go more than a couple blocks off . . . and stick together. If anybody got separated, it could be real tough."

"Vasana says it's real close."

"Sure. Have a good time."

After changing into more casual clothes, Bucky met the two girls in front of the hospital. "Where to?"

"Down here." Weaving through the crowded

sidewalk traffic, Vasana led the two Americans to a large walled-in compound where tourists and nationals alike crowded together.

"What's in there?" Bucky craned his head.

"Many Buddha figures," Vasana said solemnly. "Many people come to worship here."

The smell of incense was strong in the air as the three students slipped into the main temple. Rows and rows of shoes lined the entrance.

"Do we . . ."

"Yes." Vasana reached down and unbuckled her sandals, signaling the others to do the same.

Fascinated, Bucky watched as the Thais reverently knelt and meditated in front of the huge golden Buddha sitting stolidly at the front of the temple. One small woman, gray hair pulled back into a tiny bun, held trembling hands together in prayer, rocking slowly back and forth.

"Do they really think that he can answer their prayers?" Bucky whispered.

Vasana nodded slowly. "Some, yes. Others think, 'Buddha is dead but his words are good for people to live by.' "

"What about, you know, sin and someone dying for them and everything like that?"

"No. Buddhism has nothing like that."

"Are most people here Buddhists?"

"Almost all." Vasana gave Noelle's sleeve a little tug, indicating it was time to go. "There are few Christians in Thailand."

Bucky thought about a recent *Insight* article that had described the Adventist Church's goals of penetrating every culture in the world with the gospel. The images of those hundreds of worshipers bowing low to a dust-covered piece of gold troubled him the rest of the day.

* * *

That evening the hospital bus drove the group down to one of Bangkok's busiest sections of town. Milling crowds jostled the teens as they gawked at the crowded shops and street vendors.

"Man, look at all these movies!" Benny pointed to a booth where all the latest American video hits were on display. He pointed to one. *"Tao rai?"*

The diminutive salesman brightened. "One hundred baht."

"Man, four bucks for a video. How do they do it?"

Gordon gave Benny a nudge. "It's all pirated stuff," he murmured.

"Stolen?"

"May as well be." He gestured at the rows of tapes. "Somebody takes a U.S. film and just cranks out a hundred copies with video equipment. Then sells 'em out here for four or five bucks each. Problem is, it's all illegal. The movie company, producers, nobody back home gets the royalties they're supposed to." He pointed toward another stall. "Same with music cassettes. A buck apiece, all pirated."

"Man." Benny shook his head. "'Course, I don't feel bad much for the movie companies. They got plenty of money, but it still ain't right."

"Yeah. Come on, let's eat." Bucky tugged at his friend's shirt sleeve.

Minutes later the students were seated at three booths in one of Bangkok's finest Pizza Hut restaurants. "Home sweet home," Ricki announced as she took a huge bite of her cheese/olive/pineapple special deluxe.

"Seems dumb to fly all the way out to Thailand and then eat at Pizza Hut," Bucky grinned.

"After a week in the jungle, some good old American food sounds just fine to me." Benny rubbed his hands together as the little Thai waitress slid a big pizza in front of him. "Thank you, honey."

"You're welcome." The restaurant employee had been carefully trained to reply in the appropriate English expressions, Bucky noticed.

Gordon came over to where the boys were gulping down their fast-food meal. Behind him was a young Thai man with a confident smile. "Listen, fellows, I want you to meet Chai. He's a lab technician at the hospital here."

"How ya doin'?" The boys responded in chorus.

"Chai tells me there's a Thai boxing match over at some stadium near here that's very interesting. Costs about a dollar to get in, and it's quite an exhibition. You know, kind of like martial arts—kick-boxing and everything. He wants to know if any of you are interested."

"Yeah!" Benny, of course, was the first to speak. He looked over at Bucky. "What about it, Stone?"

Bucky glanced to where Vasana was eating with two of her friends. "I . . . don't know."

"Come on, man. This is Thailand. Let's see some Thai boxing." He feinted with his left fist. "Don't make me have to persuade you."

With a sigh, Bucky nodded. "Yeah, sure. I'll go."

"All right!" Benny scanned the row of boys. "Any of you other guys want to go?"

Carl shook his head. "I don't know. What are the rest doing?"

Gordon signaled for the bill before answering.

"Oh, just looking around right here. There's lot of little street shops and everything. We've got to stay real close to the bus so we don't get separated."

"I think I'll do that."

Benny wadded up his napkin. "Nobody else? Bucky, I guess it's just you and me and . . . what was your name?"

"Chai." The older student spoke with a pronounced accent.

"Let's check it out."

"Now wait a minute." Gordon put a hand on Chai's shoulder. "You three guys stick close together. This is a big, mean city, 'specially at night. I don't want anybody getting lost. Chai, you're sure the three of you can get back to the hospital without any problem."

"Oh, yes. Bus ride to hospital is very simple. City bus, three baht."

"Hey," Benny said easily, "anything goes wrong, I just hop in a taxi and say, 'Take me to *roang payaban mitchun*.' Mission Hospital."

The youth director glanced at Chai. "Well, keep these two guys right with you. They don't know the language, so . . ." He gave the Thai student a pointed look.

"Yes, yes." The young man's head bobbed in agreement. "We will stay together."

NINE

THAI BOXING

The crowd roared in frenzy as the two wiry athletes in the ring darted and jabbed at each other. *Bam!* With a swift kick, the Thai in the red trunks sent his opponent staggering.

"They can really do that?" Bucky couldn't believe his eyes.

"Yes, Thai boxing rules very different from U.S.A." Chai took a sip of his soda.

The red-trunked attacker bore in hard, but with a flurry of stinging jabs, his rival drove him away. A second cheer went up at the counterattack. A group of Thais sitting nearby jabbered excitedly among themselves, passing bills back and forth.

"What are they doing?"

Chai eyed the men. "Betting, I think."

The atmosphere in the stadium was electrifying, almost intoxicating. The smell of Thai beer was heavy in the air. Bucky shifted uncomfortably in his seat.

"Dhai lao!" A shriek went up from a man near the front as one of the boxers staggered and fell heavily. The fan rose to his feet, gesturing excitedly in victory.

"Is that it?" Bucky turned to Chai, hoping the bout was over.

"Yes. First match only. Two more to go."

Bucky winced. "Listen, I . . ."

"What's the matter, Stone?" Benny craned to see the referee indicating the winner. "You OK?"

Shaking his head, Bucky said, "Man, I don't like this."

"How come?"

"I . . . well, look, it's awfully violent and everything. Plus half the people here are drunk. Look around."

Benny started to say something, then nodded reluctantly. "Yeah, I guess you're right." He turned to Chai. "What do you say, Chai? Let's go."

The Thai glanced at the ring where two new fighters were being introduced to applause. "Good fight coming," he said hopefully.

"Yeah, but we just . . . we're just not into it." Benny tried to be diplomatic. "Look, let's go for some ice cream or something. I'm buyin', boys."

Bucky gave his friend a thankful look.

Outside Lumpini Stadium the air was cool and clear, free from the heavy cloud of tobacco smoke. Bucky took a deep breath. "Sorry," he said. "But that just wasn't . . ."

"Hey, no problem-o." Benny tried to get his bearings. "Chai, we're looking for the nearest ice cream depot. Help us out."

The Thai youth pointed to a small restaurant

across the street. "Good ice cream there."

The three young men savored the tart, creamy dessert. "You like mango ice cream?" Chai asked Bucky.

"Yeah, it's good." The young student looked in fascination at the throng of shoppers going by the outdoor restaurant. Set up near the table was a huge display of watches. "Are those any good?"

Chai shook his head. "Rolex," he laughed. "All fake. Last maybe three months. Five hundred baht."

Benny shook his head, laughing. "Man, twenty bucks for a fake Rolex. Too much!"

"Time to catch bus." Chai finished his ice cream cone and beckoned to the others. "Over here."

Bucky quietly patted his wallet as he stood and followed the two other boys. The crowd looked harmless enough, but a tourist from California could never tell.

At the bus stop sign the boys waited along with at least 80 other people. "You sure we can get on?" Benny grinned.

"Several buses stop here," Chai responded. "Not all of them ride our bus."

"Good thing." Bucky watched as an overloaded bus rumbled by without stopping. "What about that one?"

"Not here." Chai peered to see the destination sign on the front of the bus. "Only one bus goes to hospital."

"They come along every few minutes?"

"Yes, many buses. Cars in Bangkok very expensive. So many buses."

Several went by before Chai grabbed Bucky's arm. "This one."

The American boy gasped. The overloaded vehicle was absolutely jammed with humanity. A mass of bodies filled the aisles and spilled out onto the loading steps at the rear of the bus.

"We'll never get on," Benny declared.

"No." Even Chai could see it was hopeless. "Wait for next bus."

Bucky had to laugh. "I've never seen anything like that before in my life."

Idly he glanced down the street as they waited. Huge neon signs everywhere flickered in intricate designs. Glowing lights chased each other around the border of a billboard advertising Budweiser. Across the street a huge theater marquee featured 40-foot movie characters from a film he recognized as a hit in the U.S. two years earlier.

"Now we go!" Chai whistled to him. "Another bus!"

Bucky turned quickly as the diesel bus lurched to a stop. "Still too full!" he complained.

"No, this one good." Chai pushed Benny ahead of him and turned to make sure Bucky was right behind. "Hurry!"

Wedging his way through the pile of bodies standing in the doorway, Benny clambered on. Chai grabbed the handrail and pulled himself on board.

Just as Bucky climbed onto the first step, something sharp hit him right in the forehead. With an involuntary gasp, he stepped back for a moment, dazed. A tall Thai youth, in a hurry to get aboard, rubbed his elbow nonchalantly and muttered something to the ticket girl.

"Wait!" Bucky lunged for the door railing, but the painful blow had left him reeling. With grinding gears the overloaded bus began to pull away from the curb.

"I'm not on!" Despite the pain, Bucky began to run toward the receding lights, but a sea of humanity blocked his path. Pushing through a knot of four giggling students, he dashed toward the back of the bus that was rapidly picking up speed.

A feeling of terror seized him. The usual mass of traffic had temporarily let up, and the city bus with Benny and Chai on board was now turning the corner at the intersection well down the street.

His head pounded. *What should I do?* For an irrational moment he still considered running after the bus, hoping to catch it in the next street at a traffic signal. *Should I . . . ?*

Desperate now, he actually began to sprint down the sidewalk. But he had only gone 30 yards when he realized the hopelessness of the situation. The sidewalk was thick with pedestrians blocking his way.

Real fear seized him as he slowly returned to the bus stop. He studied the sign on the front of a second bus now pulling to a stop at the curb. Was it the same line? Staring at the foreign letters, he grimaced.

"Why didn't I ask Chai what number bus it was?" he muttered to himself in frustrated rage.

Screwing up his courage, he paused next to a young man. "Does this bus go to the Adventist hospital?"

The student turned to his friend with a shrug, then laughed.

"I'm lost." Bucky tried to slow down his racing pulse. "Do you speak English?"

The second student cackled. "Hello, Joe."

"You do?"

Another laugh. "No, Joe."

A second bus swung into loading position right behind the first one. Again Bucky sized it up, realizing with fresh despair how alike they all looked.

At last he realized the truth. The best thing to do was wait, hoping that Chai and Benny, recognizing that he was missing, would return to the bus stop.

Pacing back and forth, he watched as the minute hand slowly slipped around the face of his watch. Ten minutes . . . 15 . . . 20. "Come on!" Now almost trembling with fear, he muttered in frustration to himself, "Where are you guys?"

A full half hour went by before he finally gave up watching the throng of faces in the crowd in the vain hope that he would see his two friends. Slamming his fist into his open palm from frustration, he went over to a low wall surrounding a movie theater and sat down.

Almost involuntarily he began to pray. "Lord," he began, "I know *You* know where I am. Please . . . help me to think how I should get back to the hospital."

Opening his eyes, he almost expected to see the hospital bus pull up with Gordon and his 18 friends. The garish neon lights blinked out their beer promotions as the city traffic rushed by in all directions.

Taking a deep breath, he made his way over to the curb once again. Scanning the oncoming traffic carefully, he raised his hand timidly and beckoned as an empty taxi approached.

The Thai driver screeched to a halt near the young student and stubbed out a cigarette. Bucky cleared his throat. "Can you take me to the Adventist hospital?" He spoke slowly, hoping the driver would recognize the words.

The man stared at him blankly. "Adventist hospital." Bucky repeated the phrase, trying to emphasize what he wanted with a gesture.

"*Mai roo.*"

"Hospital . . . hospital." He tried to think of some kind of pantomime that would convey the idea.

"You want where?" A voice at his side interrupted.

Bucky turned. A tall man had been watching.

"You speak English?"

"Little bit."

Bucky sighed in relief. "I need the Seventh-day Adventist Hospital."

A puzzled expression crossed the man's face. "Hospital. Which one?"

"Seventh-day Adventist." Bucky paused. "SDA?"

The man seemed to comprehend. Bending down he jabbered some words in Thai. Bucky strained to hear, trying to catch any familiar phrases.

The driver nodded and responded. The man straightened up. "He says 150 baht."

Bucky winced. The amount was nearly all he had in his wallet. He remembered Benny's successful bargaining the week earlier.

"Ask him . . . if 120 is OK."

The helpful stranger spoke again in Thai, then briefly shook his head. "One-fifty."

Nodding reluctantly, Bucky climbed into the back seat. "Thank you."

"Yes, OK." The Thai man waved.

His pounding pulse rate began to slow as the taxi eased through the Saturday night traffic. The driver hummed to himself as a raucous Thai pop tune rattled in the car's tinny speakers.

Bucky stared out the window, hoping to see

anything familiar that would indicate they were heading in the right direction. Something in the back of his mind indicated that the hospital was off to the left, but he was certainly too disoriented to rely on that instinct. Still, he fretted to himself when the small taxi turned right at a huge circle intersection and headed down a street filled with bars and nightclubs.

"Lord, let this be right," he muttered to himself over and over as they rolled through intersection after intersection. In the neon-sprayed late evening nothing looked even remotely familiar.

At last the taxi slowed to a stop. A large stucco building was nearly dark. The sign above the entrance was in Thai. Gulping down his fear, Bucky poked his head out the window to scan the place.

"This isn't it," he said, shaking his head. Squinting, he made out the English lettering underneath. "Chonburi Dental Clinic."

"No," he protested to the driver. "Adventist hospital. Big." He gestured with his hands.

The driver pointed out the window at the clinic, responding with a confident statement that Bucky couldn't understand.

"No, this isn't it." His mind raced. "Adventist hospital."

The driver shook his head blankly, then shrugged.

"Adventist hospital. Big." Bucky gestured. "This little. Not right."

Again the man shook his head, this time more forcefully. He repeated the same expression.

"This isn't right!" An edge crept into Bucky's voice. "Adventist hospital."

The man reached behind him and unlatched the passenger door, allowing it to swing open.

"Wait! You didn't take me to the right place!" Bucky brought both hands down hard on the back of the driver's seat. "This isn't it!"

The man shrugged again, then held out his hand, gesturing for payment.

Shaking with anger, Bucky counted out the bills and handed them over. The slim 20-baht bill remaining reminded him just how desperate he now was.

Muttering what sounded to Bucky like an epithet, the taxi driver revved up his motor and squealed out into traffic, leaving his passenger standing on the corner in front of a dental clinic that had been closed for hours.

TEN

COCKTAIL WAITRESS

Bucky stood on the curb as the taxi melted into a distant blur of taillights. A tightening knot in his stomach felt the size of one of Coach Brayshaw's basketballs. With a dull stab of pain he realized how far away he was from home.

He glanced around him at the faces of strangers. Surrounded by people and traffic and noise, he still felt desperately, terrifyingly alone. Alone in Bangkok.

Trying to keep his hands from shaking, he walked over to the dental clinic and tried the front knob. Locked. Through the glass door he could see dim lights, but there appeared to be no one there to help.

Sitting down on the steps, he pulled out his wallet and examined its contents, knowing already that he had less than one dollar to his name. Twenty baht. Not enough for another taxi ride or even a single meal.

His mind raced. *Should I have waited at that bus stop? What if Chai and Benny are going back there right now with Gordon?* Anger and fear began to gnaw at him. *How could I have been so stupid? When you're lost, stay put! Even Rachel Marie knows that!*

He racked his brain. What was the name of the boxing stadium? Could he go to the police? How did one say the name of the Adventist hospital in Thai? In his mind he could hear Benny boastfully pronouncing the foreign words . . . something starting with "r." He strained to remember.

With a weary sigh, he stood up and began to aimlessly walk down the darkened street. Stores, bolted tight with mesh iron gates, lined the roadway. A mangy dog crossed in front of him, growling as he shied away from it.

"God, please . . ." Almost too tired to pray, he whispered the words over and over.

A car loaded with teenagers slowed down as it passed him. "Hey! *Falang!*" The mocking laughter rang in his ears as he trudged toward the intersection.

Two blocks down he spotted what looked like a more public area. Bright lights and restaurant signs flickered with the faint promise of help. The pink glow of American neon beckoned.

At the traffic light he paused. A set of railroad tracks sliced across the intersection. The red-and-white pole was just descending as a clanging bell announced the arrival of a train.

Bucky watched as the passenger cars slowly lumbered past. More irrational thoughts flooded his fatigued mind. *Would this train go right by the hospital? Should he hop on?* He shook the idea away, waiting for the bar to lift before crossing over to the crowded street on the other side.

Restaurant signs and nightclub marquees twinkled as he slowly walked down the street. "GIRLS! GIRLS! GIRLS!" a sign promised. Inside he could hear the heavy beat of an American pop tune. The familiar words pounded in his brain, reminding him again how far away America and Hampton Beach were. Halfway down the street he suddenly paused. The numbing fatigue of the last two hours had abruptly drained the last ounces of energy out of him. Sagging against the nearest wall, he glanced at his watch. Nearly midnight.

"God, I don't know what to do." It was more of a groan than a prayer.

He glanced across the street where a huge scarlet sign announced DANCES & DRINKS. Pushing himself away from the wall, he picked his way across the crowded street and walked into the darkened bar.

The nightclub was half-filled with customers watching three girls dance on a small stage. Scarcely noticing, Bucky made his way over to a distant corner of the room and sank down into a chair. The pulsating rhythm of the rock music seemed to drag strength out of him with every beat.

"What do you want?"

He jerked his head up. A smiling Thai waitress in a short miniskirt stood before him, pad poised.

"I . . . I can't . . ." His voice trailed away.

"You want drink?"

Bucky shook his head. "You speak English?"

"Yes, a little bit."

He wet his lips. "I'm lost. I was with some friends and then they got on a bus . . . and I couldn't get on

. . . and now I don't know how to get home." The words tumbled out in a confused rush.

She cocked her head. "You don't want drink? Martini? Beer?"

"No!" Grimacing in frustration, he repeated himself. "I'm lost. Please! Can you help me get home?"

The pencil dangled over the pad for just a moment, then dropped. She gave a demure shrug. "You wait."

Another rock song boomed through the huge speakers right over Bucky's head as the crowd began to sway to the beat. He pressed his hands against his forehead, trying to stop the throbbing pain that was beginning to build.

"Hello." The voice jarred him back to attention. "What's the matter, honey?" A woman in her mid-30s peered at him through her heavy makeup. She looked Asian but spoke with more of a British accent.

"I got lost." He was too tired to explain further.

"That's what my girl told me." The woman slipped into the seat next to him. "Where you from, doll?"

"California."

"A California man. My favorite." She leered at him, her heavy eyelids fluttering.

"Please . . . " He swallowed hard. "I got lost. My friends are all at the Adventist hospital."

"The what?"

"The Seventh-day Adventist hospital. It's by some railroad tracks. Real big compound, four-story building."

"Oh, sure." She put a manicured hand on his forearm. "I know where that is, honey."

"You do?" His voice trembled with excitement.

"Sure." Her laugh was silvery, mysterious. "Come on, have a drink on the house, then I'll have one of my boys drive you home."

Tired as he was, Bucky managed a grin of relief. "You don't know what this means to me."

"No problem, baby." She motioned to the waitress. "What do you like to drink?"

He was still tingling with relief. "Oh, just . . . 7-Up, I guess."

The older woman laughed out loud. "7-Up! Well, well. You *are* a big man, aren't you?" She slapped him playfully on the arm. "Come on, have a real drink."

Bucky shook his head. "No, I don't drink."

The hostess laughed again. "Well, you came to a strange place for help." She said something to the waitress in Thai, then slipped out of her chair. "Well, you're a good-looking California boy so far away from home. Too bad you're not the party type." She gave him a mocking glance.

A minute later the waitress returned with a tall glass of icy liquid. "Here you are, baby doll," the hostess rasped, giving Bucky a wink. "Drink up, then we'll get you back home to Mommy." She laughed again.

Bucky gulped gratefully at the cold soda. *Home. Safe on the hospital compound in Dr. Geltje's apartment. Then California.* At that moment the twin destinations seemed like heaven to him.

As he glanced down at his nearly empty glass, he thought the familiar soda had a tart flavor to it.

Despite his near exhaustion, he felt a momentary sense of anticipation that the hours of fear were at last coming to an end.

The heavily painted hostess eyed him for a moment, then went over to the bar and whispered to a stocky bartender. Bucky drained the last drops of liquid from his glass as he listened to the frantic music. Somehow the tune's heavy beat had a mushy quality to it. *Moosh . . . moosh . . . moosh*. The garbled lyrics rumbled in his brain as the scantily-clad dancers gyrated on the stage.

Glancing at his watch, he squinted in the darkness to see the hands. Suddenly it was an effort to focus. Rubbing at his eyes, he looked up at the stage again. Now there were six dancers there . . . no, it was only three. Or was it? His eyes seemed to be twitching.

"How're you feeling, honey?" The woman's voice barely penetrated his drowsiness.

"I . . . I can't seem to. . ." His tongue was thick. "I'm so . . ."

Through the rose-colored murky darkness he could hear the mocking sound of her laughter as he slipped into unconsciousness.

ELEVEN

THE LAST TRY

The hot Bangkok sun beat down on the piles of trash in the alley, bathing the block with the stench of rotting garbage. The acrid smell penetrated Bucky's sleep and jerked him to a painful consciousness.

"What? . . ."

Coughing violently, he looked at his dingy surroundings. A dog nibbled at some half-eaten fruit that had fallen out of a paper sack. Out on the main street cars and motor scooters whizzed past, their engines a high, piercing whine.

Bucky tried to stagger to his feet, only to have his legs, buckled under him for who knew how long, tingle painfully as the circulation began to flow again.

"Where am I?" He half-spoke the words as he gazed jerkily around the alley. Despite the mid-morning glare, he could barely open his eyelids.

Forcing himself to sit back down, he began thinking furiously. The bar, the flirtatious hostess, the drink . . .

The drink! With a start, he remembered the blurred vision, the distant laughter. Despite his pounding headache, he could recall now the slow descent into a drugged sleep.

All at once he remembered a story he'd read in a travel guide. His breath came in angry little gasps as he felt for his wallet. The empty fabric of his back pocket confirmed his suspicion.

"*Drugged!*" Indignantly he struggled to his feet, his head reeling from the movement. Putting his hands on his knees, he bent over for a moment, allowing the blood flow to ease the dizziness.

"Where am I?" he mumbled to himself. Straining to recover the bits of memory, he pieced the puzzle together. The boxing match . . . missed bus . . . the taxi ride to the dental clinic . . . the walk to the bar.

"Sunday morning in Bangkok." He muttered the words aloud, trying desperately to regain a measure of thoughtful calm. "And no wallet."

Despite his aching limbs, his mouth twisted into a wry grin as he thought of the robbers' frustration at finding only 20 baht in his wallet. Then his anger returned. *How could they!*

Picking his way through the reeking mounds of trash he headed for the main street where he stared in both directions. Nothing looked familiar.

"Where's that bar?" Gingerly moving through the foot traffic, he walked down the block, studying both sides of the street. Without the neon glow everything looked different anyway, but after walking just to the first corner he realized he was in a completely different part of town.

"They must have taken my money and then dumped me way over here," he grumbled to himself, biting his lip to keep from spitting out his rage. Crude profanities from his early days in public junior high school crowded his mind.

At the next corner he paused and looked in every direction. A painful hunger began to twist at his insides, adding to the queasiness already there. The last traces of the drug must still be in his system, he decided.

Halfway down the next block was a bus stop with a long wooden bench. A metal roof and walls, plastered with Thai advertising posters, provided at least some protection from the sun. Bucky sank down wearily on the edge of the bench, ignoring the curious stares of Thai students.

Where to? Bucky realized that the old adage about "Stay put when you're lost" no longer applied. He was miles removed from any place his friends might be looking for him. Sitting quietly on the bench for 15 minutes, he tried to sort out his jumbled thoughts.

But nothing came to mind. Finally, sighing heavily, he picked himself up and began to walk down the street once again. Somewhere in this huge Asian city was that quiet, walled compound from where he hoped 18 friends and Pastor Gordon were looking for him.

He walked two more blocks before stopping again. A small restaurant with English lettering on it attracted his attention. He pushed his way into the quiet interior and went up to the cash register.

"Hello." The woman spoke the greeting tentatively.

"You speak English?"

"No. Only little."

Bucky took a deep breath. "Do you know where the Adventist hospital is?" Even to him the simple words sounded complicated now.

"Hospital, no. This restaurant."

"I know." He rubbed at his eyes. "I need Adventist hospital. Seventh-day Adventist." He thought hard. "SDA?"

The woman shook her head sympathetically. "*Mai kowchai.*" She gave a little shrug.

"Don't understand. Yeah." Sighing, he motioned with his hand. "Drink? Water?" Reluctantly he forced Gordon's health warnings from his mind.

She nodded, filling a grimy cup with water from a faucet and handing it to him. Bucky's stomach tightened as he forced the liquid down.

Setting the cup back on the counter, he looked at the woman again. "Bathroom? I need a bathroom." He could think of no way to explain his need except to speak clearly and hope she understood. "Bathroom?"

The woman lifted her hands in friendly helplessness. "Doan know," she replied in broken English.

Bucky nodded wearily. "Thanks."

"Goodbye," she said, picking up the cup and putting it back in place.

The rising temperature outside hit him like a boxer's blow. He trembled involuntarily. The painful hunger and his urgent need for a restroom were causing real agony now.

He trudged two more blocks, pausing once to ask

a well-dressed man if he knew where the Adventist hospital was. A short, staccato laugh and shake of the head were his only response.

Suddenly Bucky brightened. Way down the street, nearly three blocks away, was a familiar yellow. "Wendy's! It's a Wendy's!" In his eagerness he darted forward, dodging the hurtling cars as he crossed the intersections.

The air-conditioned breeze bathed his perspiring face as he entered the familiar fast-food restaurant. A huge menu announced a smorgasbord of American items and their Thai equivalents, along with prices in baht.

Slipping into the men's room, he sank down to rest in one of the stalls. Minutes later he emerged with his face clean and toweled off. Standing in line, he waited impatiently until he reached the counter.

"Hello. May I please help you?" The waitress was a tall Thai girl, dressed in the familiar Wendy's outfit. She parroted the phrase carefully.

"I need . . . is the manager here?"

The girl's forehead furrowed as she digested the words. "Not today," she said at last. "Tomorrow he is here."

"I need someone to help me. I got lost."

"You want food? May I help you?"

The same familiar frustration began to rise again. *Why can't anybody understand me!* The week of goodwill and love for the Thai people began to slip away. He forced the irrational anger from his mind.

"I got lost. I have no money. I need to find the Adventist hospital." He recited the words with a numb sliver of hope.

"I don't know . . . you . . . what you say." The girl

shrugged, motioning to a fellow employee.

"Yes. May I help you?"

Bucky repeated the words to the boy. "I need someone to help me."

The same shrug. "Manager not here. You want order? No?"

"I don't have any money!" The words came out more sharply than Bucky intended. Taking a deep breath, he forced himself to be calmer. "Somebody took all my money. I'm broke . . . and lost . . . and nobody seems to be able to help me."

The two Wendys' employees glanced at each other helplessly. "I don't know how you . . . what . . ." The boy's English faded into a silent stare.

Bucky nodded wearily as he turned and went out. Outside two huge buses rumbled past the American-style restaurant, their seats and aisles jammed with passengers.

Could I call the hospital? The thought popped into his brain as he remembered the switchboard operator in the lobby of the Adventist hospital. Searching up and down the street, he recalled now that in nearly two weeks in Thailand he hadn't seen a single pay phone.

"Plus you haven't got any money, dodo," he reminded himself, thrusting his hands into his pockets as he began walking down the street.

No phones. No police. His mind bounced from idea to idea, rejecting each one almost instantly. *Bangkok was just a whole different kind of place when you were lost,* he grimaced.

During a temporary lull in the frantic rush-hour traffic, three empty taxis zipped past, each one seemingly trying to outrace the others to the next red light.

Chewing his lip as he thought, Bucky suddenly stopped in mid-stride and stepped to the curb. An idea was beginning to form.

Almost immediately a taxi scooted up next to him. The driver nodded affably without speaking, waiting for instructions. Knowing it was unlikely that the man would understand, Bucky still repeated his request for help in getting to the Adventist hospital.

The taxi driver shook his head. *"Mai kowchai."*

By now the negative response needed no explanation. Just to be sure, Bucky repeated the destination once more. "Hospital. Adventist. Seventh-day Adventist."

Another determined shake.

The teenage boy took a deep breath. "Christian church," he said simply. "Christian church." The driver thought for a moment, digesting the words. "Christian church," Bucky repeated. He put his hands together in a worshipful manner. "Christian."

A hopeful gleam came into the man's eyes. "Chlistian," he lisped.

"Yes! Yes! Christian church. Can you take me?"

The man pondered, then nodded, looking at him curiously. "Hundred baht."

His pockets empty, Bucky nodded in agreement and climbed in. "This better work, Lord," he breathed as the taxi sped into traffic and raced to beat a yellow light.

The pain in his stomach was a dull ache now as he watched the crowded scenery slip by. Once he thought he recognized the bar from the night before, but it was impossible to tell with so many buses and heavily-loaded trucks blocking the view.

The taxi abruptly turned right, squealing in front of

an oncoming van filled with construction workers. "Watch it!" Bucky gulped.

The driver grumbled something in Thai without looking back at his passenger. Easing the cab over to the sidewalk, he pointed at a medium-size building on the left.

Bucky peered out the window at the sign. "Assembly of God Congregation," he read.

"OK?" The cabbie looked at him for approval.

The young man took a deep breath. "Yeah, OK," he said slowly. Tugging on the door's latch, he stepped out and paused by the cabbie's window. "You wait here," he said, trying to make each word clear.

"Hundred baht," the man reminded.

"I know." Bucky tried to sound placating. "Just a minute. You wait here." He pointed at his watch. "Two minutes, OK?"

A pause. "OK."

Hoping against hope, Bucky went up to the door and knocked. For a moment there was an almost excruciating silence. He knocked again.

A female voice inside called out something in Thai. He could hear footsteps approaching.

"Please, Lord . . ."

The door swung open. A cheerful Thai woman, wearing a plain cotton dress with tiny matching earrings, looked at him curiously. "Yes?"

"You speak English?"

"Not so much. Just one moment, please."
She left abruptly and went into the next room. Bucky could hear a phone ringing. He turned to where the taxi driver was waiting, breathing another wordless prayer as he did so.

"May we help you?" An American man, wearing a short-sleeved white shirt and no tie, stood at the door.

Bucky felt emotion flooding his eyes. "Yeah," he managed. "I'm lost . . . and broke. I need to get to the Adventist hospital." The words, spoken for what seemed to him like the thousandth time, tingled with new hope.

"How'd you get here?" The pastor's voice was friendly.

Bucky nodded wearily toward the cab. "He brought me here. I've got to give him a hundred baht, but I'm broke. Somebody took my money last night. If you can just get me to the Adventist hospital, I've got money there. And all my friends." His words came in fatigued little bursts. "Do you know where the Adventist hospital is?"

The words hung in the air. At that moment Bucky felt like one more no would be the final straw.

The pastor laughed. "Sure." He looked over at his Thai secretary.

"Really?"

Another laugh. "Every Christmas we get together with them and do a concert. Us, them, and the Baptists. Sure, I know where they are. My wife had an emergency root canal job done there last month."

Tears of relief sprang into Bucky's eyes. "If you could get me home, I just . . ." His knees felt weak.

The Assembly of God minister put a hand on Bucky's shoulder. "Let me get your taxi man taken care of first," he said. "Then we'll see about getting you home to your friends."

TWELVE

REUNION

Dazed, Bucky watched as the tall minister went out to where the taxi driver waited impatiently. Fishing in his pocket, the man pulled out a red bill and handed it to the cabbie, who grunted and gunned his engine in response.

"What's your name?" the pastor asked as he came back up the walk.

"Bucky. Bucky Stone."

The kind-looking man eyed him. "You look pretty banged up. Have you had anything to eat?"

Wearily the teenager shook his head. "Not since last night."

"What happened to you anyway?" He motioned him into a small kitchen next to his study. "Let's see what we've got here." He pulled out a plate of pineapple slices and some bread. "Here, have some of this."

Over the cold fruit and pieces of bread spread with homemade coconut honey, Bucky told his story. The minister whistled as Bucky described being drugged in the bar. "No kidding! What a mess!"

The man looked at him thoughtfully. "You realize how lucky you are to be alive."

"I know."

"Places like that rip people off all the time. Bangkok is fierce for stuff like that. I'd think if they found somebody with a lousy 20 baht in his pocket, they'd just as soon put a bullet in him as anything."

Bucky trembled. "All I know is, I woke up this morning with a headache and no money."

The minister nodded. "I guess I never introduced myself." He held out his hand. "Reverend Thomas. Gerald Thomas."

Bucky wiped some honey off his fingers and shook hands. "I can't tell you how much this means to me," he said fervently.

"No problem. Your Adventist friends here in Bangkok are pretty good people. I'm happy to do a favor any time for you all."

"Well," Bucky sighed in relief, "they're going to be awfully relieved when we get there."

Pastor Thomas smiled. "What do you say we do just that?"

The same frantic traffic rumbled by as the young minister guided them through busy intersections in his little blue Mazda. Somehow the foreign harshness of Bucky's surroundings now seemed friendly again. "Sure feels good to know I'm out of this mess," he murmured.

"Well, the Lord had his eye on you, son." The pastor glanced in his rear view mirror before switching lanes. " 'Cause you were a long way from your hospital."

"Is that it up there?" Bucky spied the railroad crossing and the familiar concrete wall.

"Sure is."

"Boy, I was starting to think I'd never see it again."

"When do you head back to the States?"

"Tomorrow." Bucky looked over at his new friend. "How long have you been out here?"

"Just about two years. I got two more before my first term is up. My wife and I came here from Seattle. She teaches English at our language school."

"You like it out here?"

"I sure do." Pastor Thomas pulled to a stop as the railroad crossing bars slowly dropped, blocking the traffic. "The people are wonderful here, and now that I'm learning the language, witnessing for God is a real thrill."

"You speak Thai?"

A laugh. "*Nit noi.*"

"What's that mean?"

" 'Little bit.' "

Bucky watched the passenger train creak by. "How do you say the name of the Adventist hospital in Thai?"

The pastor squinted. "Seems like everybody calls it the Mission Hospital. *'Roang payaban mitchun'—something like that."*

"That's it!" The painfully elusive phrase seemed so easy now. "Man, all morning I couldn't think of it."

"And here we are." Pastor Thomas wheeled into the front entrance and slowed down. "Where do you think your friends are?"

"I don't know." Bucky looked at the hospital's

main lobby. "Let's try in here, I guess." Suddenly he gasped. "There! Right there's Pastor Humboldt!"

The little Mazda lurched to a stop. "This I've got to see!" the pastor grinned.

Climbing out of the car, Bucky bounded toward the entrance where Gordon was frantically gesturing to three Thai men. One of them was wearing some kind of khaki uniform and pointing at a large map.

"Gordon!" The teenager's voice shook.

The youth director whirled at the sound. His face grew slack as he spotted the American boy. "Bucky!" Dashing toward him, the man enveloped him in a huge hug. "Oh, God, thank You!" Then he clutched at Bucky, pounding him happily on the back over and over.

The three men gathered around them, jabbering excitedly. "This him?" one of them asked in his rudimentary English.

"Yes! Yes! He's home!" Gordon's voice shook with emotion. Standing a few yards away, Pastor Thomas watched with a thoughtful smile. Remembering the Assembly of God minister, Bucky pulled the youth director toward him.

"I guess I'd better introduce you." Disengaging himself from Gordon's embrace with a grin, he explained who Pastor Thomas was.

"Great to meet you," Gordon said, fatigue showing in his bloodshot eyes. "And, boy, thanks for your help. We were really worried."

"Praise the Lord." The Assembly of God minister put an arm around Bucky. "I guess you folks were probably up all night."

"You don't know the half of it," Gordon smiled wearily, clasping his fellow pastor's hand again.

"Between looking and praying, it was a long night and day." He glanced at Bucky. "What happened anyway?"

For the second time the young student missionary related his experience. When he began to describe his second thoughts about leaving the bus stop near the boxing stadium, the youth director shook his head in frustration.

"Yep, that's what you shoulda done. Stay right there. Chai and Benny and I went right back there and looked for almost two hours. Then we just didn't know what else to do. We contacted the police, but in a city this size, that was almost for sure not going to turn up anything."

One of the Thai men listening bobbed his head in agreement. "*Chokedee,*" he began repeating over and over.

"What's that mean?"

"Lucky. Fortunate." Pastor Thomas translated the Thai expression. "You sure were, Bucky."

"Most of the students were up praying just about all night, Bucky." Gordon pulled out a soiled white handkerchief and mopped at his nose, sneezing violently. "We just didn't have a thing to go on . . . once we couldn't find you back at that bus stop."

"Yeah, that was dumb of me," Bucky admitted. "The whole thing was stupid. Going to that boxing match, and then not staying close to Chai and Benny —"

"Chai feels terrible about the whole thing," Gordon interjected. "He kept saying you were right behind him getting on the bus, and then it was so crowded he couldn't see you. Then when it came time to get off, you weren't there."

"Hey, it's not his fault." Bucky shook his head vehemently. "Nobody's fault but my own. I really blew it. If I'd followed your instructions better, this wouldn't have happened. And then to leave that place . . . I just was scared and didn't think."

"Well, listen, fellows, the good news is that God brought Bucky back safe and sound," Pastor Thomas cut in. "It was just one of those freak things, and God had His hand over you, son."

"He sure did." Gordon Humboldt looked at the other pastor with deep gratitude. "What you did just means the world to us. And to me personally." He put an arm around the other man. "Thanks so much." He licked his lips. "What group did you say you were with?"

"Assembly of God. We've got a congregation of about 300 here in Bangkok."

"Is that right? I went to the Holy Land and roomed with one of your pastors, oh, about four years ago. Great experience."

Pastor Thomas grinned. "I was telling Bucky we team up with you Adventists every Christmas and do a concert. Sometimes we go around to the big hotels and sing carols in their ballrooms for the rich American tourists who are over here in Bangkok during the holiday." Everybody laughed.

"Oh!" Bucky suddenly remembered something. "Gordon, I need to . . . I mean, Pastor Thomas paid my taxi for me. A hundred baht. All my money's up in Dr. Geltje's place. Could you loan some to me?"

"Oh, no," the visiting pastor protested. "Don't worry about it."

"Hey, we insist." Gordon dug out his wallet and pulled free a red 100-baht bill, handing it to Pastor

Thomas. "Right now the way I feel I'd give you a hundred times that amount. You ought to stick around and let me buy you dinner before we all take off."

"Let me guess . . . one of your vegetarian specials, right?" The Assembly of God minister laughed heartily.

"You know us too well!" Despite his all-night vigil, Gordon's eyes glowed with enthusiasm.

"Bucky!" With feminine screams a group of students burst into the hospital lobby and embraced him. "Somchai just told us you were back!" One by one they hugged him. Several of the girls had been crying, Bucky noticed. Vasana, standing near the back of the knot of young people, was the last one to embrace him, her soft cheek buried against his shoulder in a lingering hug.

"Nice bunch of kids." Pastor Thomas murmured to Gordon.

"Yeah, they've been real special." The youth director dabbed at his eyes. "And I'm sure glad to have 18 of 'em again."

"Well, listen, I've got to get goin'. Sunday's our big day, you know."

"Let me walk you to your car."

Pastor Thomas waved. "'Bye, kids." He shook hands with Bucky, then, with a grin, gave him a huge bear hug. "That's how we do it in our church."

"Sounds good to me." Bucky said goodbye to his new friend, with Vasana's slim arm still around his waist.

"Who is that guy?" The usually boisterous Ricki murmured in Bucky's ear.

He grinned. "Long story."

A matronly woman came up to the little group of

students. "This is Bucky Stone?"

"Yes." Gordon clapped Bucky on the back. "Safe and sound, thank God."

"We are so glad you are all right," the hospital employee nodded. "And I have a letter for you."

"For me?"

"Yes. It came yesterday from California."

Bucky looked at the familiar handwriting on the envelope. Mom. Tears glistened in his eyes as he tore the envelope open.

"From your folks?"

Bucky nodded as he read his mother's words. "I don't know if this will reach you, Bucky, before you leave to come back home. Pastor Jensen found the address of the Adventist hospital there and gave it to me. But whether it does or not, you've been in my prayers each day while you were gone. I know God will look after you and bring you home safely. I love you so much."

There was more, but Bucky could not read it then. His lips began to quiver as he thought about his mother praying quietly in her room back home in Hampton Beach. Holding Rachel Marie in her lap while the two of them prayed for him. His hand fell to his side as he let the tears slide down his face. Vasana, watching quietly, took him by the arm and led him down the hallway away from the group, who stood silently watching the pair.

THIRTEEN

SAFELY HOME

That evening, after a meal of homemade vegeburgers, all 18 student missionaries crowded into Dr. Geltje's small living room for worship. The Danish dentist beamed as she listened to the lively youth songs Gordon strummed on his guitar.

"We used to sing like this when I was a girl," she mused. "My father played an instrument like your guitar, I remember. So well he played it."

"These same songs?" For the first time since the night before, Gordon's eyes had their familiar twinkle.

"Oh, well, no." The dentist laughed. "The old favorites. I always remember, 'Jesus, Keep Me Near the Cross.' "

"Well, hey, we can do a golden oldie, 'specially if it's that one." Bucky joined in with the others on the time-honored chorus.

As the last notes died away, Gordon looked

around at the group, his face suddenly sober. "Kids, you know what we've been through these last 24 hours." Benny draped an arm around Bucky's shoulders as the youth director quietly reflected.

"I just feel like we should sing 'God Is So Good.' No guitar, just each of us pouring out our hearts as we sing."

"Yeah." Jo-Jo, the playful one, was looking down at her tennis shoes, her eyes moist.

The a cappella music vibrated the small apartment as the boys filled in the bass parts of the song. "God is so good . . . He's coming back . . ."

After a short pause, the youth director suddenly began singing again: "He rescued me, He rescued me . . ." He glanced at Bucky. The students picked up the words, closing with a final "God is so good," that faded into silence. Outside they could hear the quiet hum of crickets in the trees surrounding Dr. Geltje's apartment.

"Better get some rest, guys," Gordon advised after they finished their prayer circle. "We gotta get up at 4:30 tomorrow morning to get to the airport on time." He forced a smile. "And most of you are already behind on sleep because of last night."

"Yeah!" Benny gave Bucky a friendly pop on the skull. "All because of you, ding-dong."

Bucky had to laugh. "Hey, what happened to all that spiritual glow and love you had for me two seconds ago?"

"Statute of limitations just ran out, sucker." Benny's big laugh almost rattled the windows. He lifted up Bucky's arm to glance at his watch. "I'm just going to beat somebody in one game of Rook before I go to sleep." He looked around the room. "Who's it gonna be?"

* * *

The big Delta jet gleamed in the Bangkok sunlight the next morning. Still tired from his experience, Bucky wandered aimlessly through the duty-free shops at the terminal as he waited for the flight to be called.

Vasana came up to him. "Ready?"

He nodded, a tiny smile on his face. "Yeah." He looked at her. "Time to go home."

The long rows of blue seats stretching to the very rear of the DC-10 were already serviced with pillows and neatly folded blankets for the trans-Pacific journey home as they boarded. Bucky, who had wrangled a seat trade so he could sit next to Vasana, buckled his belt and glanced at her. "It's sure been great getting to know you on this trip."

She made a little face at him that oddly looked very American. "It sounds like you are saying good-bye when we still have many hours of flying to do."

"That's true." He reached out and squeezed her hand for just a second. "I'm glad."

Gordon came walking through the cabin, mentally counting heads. "Yeah, we're all here," Bucky grinned.

The youth pastor looked at the couple with a smile. "You guys behave yourselves back here."

"We will." Bucky folded his hands in his lap and fixed a pious expression on his face. "I promise."

"Flying from here to the States, we'll have a real short night," Gordon reminded everybody. "'Cause we're flying west to east. Just the opposite of when we came out. And when the sun comes up tomorrow morning, it'll be Monday again."

"Two Mondays. That's the pits." Benny propped himself up, leaning against the seat in front of him as he looked around. The plane's PA system crackled as the English and Thai announcements signaled the beginning of the journey home.

* * *

The plane filled up as they made stops in Taiwan and then Seoul. Bucky and Vasana walked through the Korean air terminal, pausing to watch an American baseball game being broadcast on a huge color TV. "Wow, I guess I'll come be a missionary here," he told the Thai girl. "Wouldn't miss a thing." He winced as a Dodger clubbed a three-run homer.

The DC-10 was wall-to-wall people for the long final leg across the Pacific Ocean. Bucky and Vasana listened, fascinated, as foreign conversations went on all around them during dinner. Every now and then a familiar Thai word would penetrate the buzz. Vasana, leaning closer, patiently translated the phrases.

The cabin quieted down as evening surrounded the plane. Their little corner illuminated by a single dome light, the couple talked quietly, sharing their college plans and career hopes. He realized anew what a fascinating and uniquely thoughtful person the Thai girl was.

"I hope I can see you again sometime," he said, thinking ahead to the coming school year at Hampton Beach High. "I know L.A.'s a long ways away, but . . ."

She looked up at him, her large brown eyes not blinking. "Yes, Bucky. I . . . wish so too." Her slim hand slipped into his.

Twilight turned into an inky darkness as the flight

crew turned down the cabin lights. An old gangster film flickered on the widebody jet's four movie screens, but Bucky was too tired to pay any attention. He fell asleep with his stereo headphones still on, an old pop hit repeating over and over in his mind from the entertainment soundtrack. *I'm so glad I'm livin' in the U.S.A. . . .* Vasana dozed next to him, her head resting on his shoulder.

A Delta stewardess easing her way down the aisle noticed when he stirred. "May I get you anything?" she whispered.

Starting to shake his head, he then changed his mind. "Yeah, a 7-Up if you've got it. Diet."

A minute later she returned with the can and cup of ice. "Here you are." She paused. "What were you kids all doing out in Bangkok?"

Speaking softly so as to not waken Vasana, Bucky explained the mission trip's purpose. "Adventists run a whole bunch of these all around the world, so I decided to try one."

"Pretty good." The stewardess glanced around, but most of the passengers were either asleep or watching the second film. "I don't know much about Adventists, though. What kind of a church is it?"

In just a few sentences Bucky described the denomination, feeling a tingle of pride as he summarized the church's main beliefs. "It's a great religion," he added. "My mom and I joined about four years ago. We really like it."

"Interesting," she commented. "I grew up Methodist, but, you know, when you fly these crazy schedules, it's pretty hard to keep up with church and all."

"Yeah." Bucky nodded. "But it's pretty important stuff."

The stewardess nodded. "I suppose it is." She stood. "Well, good luck to you all. Have a good school year."

"Thanks." He peeled off the headphones and shifted his position slightly, trying not to disturb Vasana.

The pale red of sunrise accompanied the pilot's announcement that Portland was about an hour away. Bucky stretched and looked over at the Thai girl. "How'd you sleep?"

"Good." Vasana reached up in a dainty gesture, and brushed Bucky's hair into place. "Did you?"

"Not too bad."

A cheer went up from the loaded plane as the wheels touched down in Oregon. "U.S.A.!" a bearded college student sitting just in front of Bucky and Vasana hollered, raising a fist in the air.

Customs took only a few minutes as Bucky dutifully filled out the official form and turned it in. "You kids have a good time?" The agent took a quick look at the suitcase before closing it up.

"Yeah, we sure did."

"Terrific! Welcome home." The customs man picked up the bag and put it on the conveyor belt behind him. "That'll head right on out to Frisco with you."

Several of the students' parents were waiting at the gate to welcome the mission group home. Bucky gave the Portland kids each a hug, thanking them for their part in the two-week adventure. "Same time next summer?" one of them grinned.

"We'll see." Right now Bucky was too tired to think about it.

Hand in hand, he walked over with Vasana to the gate where her flight for L.A. was just boarding. "I guess this is it, little missionary." He looked at her.

Taking her bag from his shoulder, she gazed up at him. "I was happy to get to know you," she said simply. "Thank you, Bucky." She gave his hand a squeeze.

"Your ticket stub, miss?" A graying Delta employee reached out for her boarding pass.

"I'll see you later. I hope." Instinctively Bucky leaned over and quickly kissed her. Vasana blushed but didn't back away. "Bucky," she murmured, but there was more affection than reproach in her voice.

"'Bye." He watched as she went down the ramp toward her plane.

Picking up his duffel bag, he slowly walked toward the gate where his own plane, bound for the Bay Area, was just beginning to board. Suddenly he stopped, his heart beating faster. A girl, her face turned away from him, was just going down an escalator to the main level. Memories of evenings in Hampton Beach flickered in his mind. *Lisa?*

For a moment he almost followed the familiar figure. The girl, wearing a sweater just like one Lisa had often worn on cool California evenings, was rapidly walking away. Jumbled thoughts raced through his mind. *Lisa in Seattle? Portland? My letter to her telling her about this trip?*

"Your attention, please. Final call for Delta Flight 1712, departing for San Francisco. Now boarding all rows."

The abrupt announcement stopped him in his

tracks, and he stared down the escalator to the lower level, but the girl was gone. He paused for a moment, then headed toward the counter where an agent took his ticket.

The lush foliage of northern Oregon fell away as Delta Airlines carried Bucky home. Although he stared out the window, he did not see the landscape and the August clouds billowing beneath the wings of the DC-737. Uneasy memories of Lisa jumbled together with his last mental image of Vasana. He remembered her soft black hair resting against his shoulder during the long flight home from Thailand.

He sighed. "Life ain't never very easy," he muttered to himself as the aircraft began its descent into the sprawling Bay Area with its crowded freeways and bridges spanning the scenic ocean waterways.

Exiting the plane, he looked around. Despite the emotional twists and turns of the last 48 hours, he couldn't help but grin as he saw Dad, Mom, and Rachel Marie standing as close to the gate as they could get. Home was still home . . . and God was still leading in the life of one tired returning student missionary named Bucky Stone.

"Hi, Bucky!" Rachel Marie squealed with delight as she jumped into her big brother's arms. "What did you bring me?"

Setting his bag down, he hugged everybody. "It's great to be home."

The Bucky Stone Books

Making Waves at Hampton Beach High (book 1)

Summer's over and Hampton Beach High is going full swing. But this year's going to be different. Bucky Stone didn't get to go to academy, so he's decided to make the best of public school. And he's determined to share Christ while he's there. It's going to be a pretty radical year for everyone involved! Paper, 127 pages. US$4.95, Cdn$6.20.

Showdown at Home Plate (book 2)

It's late Friday afternoon during the championship game, and every eye is on Bucky. Should he take his turn at bat, or be true to his conviction not to play on Sabbath? Paper, 126 pages. US$4.95, Cdn$6.20.

Outcast on the Court (book 3)

When Bucky makes the basketball team, he discovers he has what it takes to help lead the Panthers to victory. But winning won't come easy for the athlete, because his fiercest opposition is coming from his own coach and team. Paper, 143 pages. US$4.95, Cdn$6.20.

Bucky's Big Break (book 4)

He's a winner in baseball and basketball. But what can Bucky do with a broken arm? His new job as a bank teller opens up all kinds of possibilities for his future—if he lives long enough to have one. One of his customers has a gun. Paper, 128 pages. US$4.95, Cdn$6.20.

Look for book 6 in the Bucky Stone series.

To order, call **1-800-765-6955** or write to ABC Mailing Service, P.O. Box 1119, Hagerstown, MD 21741. Send check or money order. Enclose applicable sales tax and 15 percent (minimum US$2.50) for postage and handling. Prices and availability subject to change without notice. Add GST in Canada.

Also by David Smith
Heaven

"I go to prepare a place for you," Jesus promised. And what a place! God tells us we simply can't imagine it all. "Eye hath not seen . . ." Still, it's fun to try. And that's what this book is all about—anticipating a heaven so real, so full of love and joy, that we can't wait to go!

David Smith turns our focus from this troubled world to a place where pain, sickness, and death shatter into obsolescence. To a life without hate, disease, goodbyes, or limitations. To the endless possibilities of fascinating things to do and see. Best of all, he gives us a foretaste of what it will be like to live in the presence of Jesus—forever!

Paper, 96 pages. US$7.95, Cdn$9.95.

To order, call **1-800-765-6955** or write to ABC Mailing Service, P.O. Box 1119, Hagerstown, MD 21741. Send check or money order. Enclose applicable sales tax and 15 percent (minimum US$2.50) for postage and handling. Prices and availability subject to change without notice. Add GST in Canada.